The Magic of Shamanism

The Healing Power of the Shamanic Journey

Arvick Baghramian

Edited by Nofit Itzhak

www.guid-publications.com

2015

The Magic of Shamanism

©2015, Guid Publicaciones
Bruc, 107, 5-2
08009 Barcelona
España

Email: guid@guid-publications.com

Design: Estudio Hache

ISBN: 978-84-943917-6-7 paperback
978-84-943917-7-4 ebook

No part of this publication may be reproduced, stored in a retrieval system, transmitted in any form or by any means, electronic, mechanical, photocopying, recording or otherwise, without the prior written permission of the copyright owner. All rights reserved. This book shall not be sold, lent, hired out or otherwise circulated without the publisher's consent.
Although the publisher entirely respects the author's text, the views expressed therein are those of the author.

www.guid-publications.com

What you always hear people say about Arvick is 'nothing in my life is like what it used to be before I met her'. A colourful and fascinating woman, with a life story that is in itself an infinite journey of healing and giving, Arvick shares her own life journey with the reader, carrying them away to fascinating worlds, which were always there, but not usually accessible to westerners. The pages of this book instil the reader with her strong belief that each and every one of us can heal our life and move it forward, to fulfil the higher calling for which we are on this earth. Arvick lives each day of her life in this way, fulfilling her calling with joy and love. The Magic of Shamanism inspires us to follow her, connect with our own power and come in touch with who we really are.

Michal Gazit - journalist, writer and workshop leader on creativity development and expression, Israel.

The ancient and modern healing practices of shamanism are explored here in a rich mix of research, practice and therapeutic work. Arvick gathers the anthropologist, the scientist, the psychotherapist, the shaman and the clients around the table for a wide-ranging and informative discussion. The daughter of a natural healer, Arvick adds personal perspective and meaning by sharing glimpses of her background and her story of learning and healing in a vivid and enjoyable way.

Arvick is a healer and teacher who embraces the mind, body and spirit in her practice, she has brought her considerable experience and her passionate curiosity to help us on this journey of exploration, which ultimately invites us to accept the potential and power of shamanic healing.

Kathy Fried - practitioner and teacher of integrative-counselling and shamanism.

Baghramian presents an excellent introduction to shamanic healing by an experienced practitioner. She movingly offers journeys of her own life and journeys with patients revealing the transformative effects they can have. She explains what traditional shamans do and shows in a touching way how she incorporates such practices into her healing work. This is a book presented with compassion, sensitivity and wisdom.

Dr Charlotte Hardman - Durham University

The Magic of Shamanism

To my mother and father, the two people who taught me how to love and give.

Contents

Acknowledgements	VII
Foreword	VIII
Introduction	XI

1 Shamanism: Basic Definitions — 1
- Origins of shamanism — 4
- Shamanism and religion — 8
- The shaman and the spirits — 10
- The shaman's universe — 13

2 The Shaman's Dream: Calling and Initiation — 19
- The call to become a shaman — 21
- Initiation crisis — 27
- Death and rebirth — 28
- Are shamans mentally ill? — 32
- The transformative power of crisis — 36
- Shaman as the wounded healer — 40
- Apprenticeship — 43

3 Gateway to the Spirits: Shamanic Worlds, Shamanic Journeys — 48
- Traversing the shamanic landscape — 49
- Gaining access to the spirit worlds — 51
- Inducing altered states of consciousness — 55
- The power place — 61
- Lower world journeys — 62
- The guardian spirit — 68
- Upper world journeys — 74
- Middle world journeys — 80
- Spontaneous journeys — 85
- Core shamanism — 87
- Shamanic rituals — 92

4 Beyond the Ego: Spirits and Spirituality — 110
- Spirit helpers — 112
- What are spirits? — 114
- Are spirits real? — 117
- Is shamanism a spiritual practice? — 123

5 The Ancient and the Modern: Shamanic Healing — 134
- Illness and healing in cross-cultural perspective — 135
- Healing in the eyes of the spirits — 145
- How shamans heal — 148
- Soul loss — 149
- Soul retrieval — 155
- Rituals to embody a soul — 162
- Power animals — 164
- Diagnostic journeys — 172
- Rattle healing — 181
- Healing from spirits of nature — 183

6 The Magic of Shamanism: The Journey as a Vehicle for Transformation — 189
- The power of imagery — 191
- Imagery and shamanism — 194
- Metaphors — 196
- Daniel — 204
- The magic of shamanic journeys — 217
- Journeys as a vehicle for transformation — 223
- The disenchantment of the world — 235

References	238
Index	245

Acknowledgements

I wish to thank all the people who have touched my life, from the moment of my birth up to this day, and especially those who chose to walk the spirit path with me. I gratefully acknowledge all my students and friends in Israel for their encouragement and support and for constantly reminding me how important it was to share this book with others. My deep appreciation goes to Jonathan Horwitz, who played a special role as my teacher and friend and who was the one to introduce me to the world of the spirits. I would also like to extend an enormous 'thank you' to my teacher, Dr Charlotte Hardman, who directed and encouraged me to write this book. My deepest thanks to Nofit Itzhak, for inspiring my creativity in the writing of this book. To her I am most grateful, for her constant support to me throughout the writing process and for generously helping me in my research. Without her I would never have completed this book. My warmest thanks to Ian Burkitt, for his gentle encouragement and constructive advice and to Nurit Ezer, who has supported me in both seen and unseen ways, giving generously both her time and love. I am grateful to Kathy Fried for her unconditional support, her honesty and sensitive judgment as a shamanic counsellor and to Jacqui Wordsworth, for relentlessly supporting me in my earlier research. My warmest thanks also to Jean Escott and Michal Gazit for their loving support.

I would like to acknowledge the many people, both young and old, who were willing to so generously share their personal journeys to make this book into what it is. And finally, I humbly give very special thanks to my guardian spirit and teachers in the non-ordinary reality who guided me, supported me and worked with me to bring this book to you.

Foreword

As far as I know, Arvick Baghramian has managed to do in this book what no other writer on shamanism has managed to do: give an overview of the shamanic literature, recount her own introduction to shamanism as an apprentice, and also speak of her experiences as a shamanic healer and one who follows the shaman's path.

As a teacher of shamanism I am often asked, is it possible for a Westerner – or for that matter anyone not born and brought up in the wilderness, whether it be in the Siberian arctic, the Amazonian rain forest, or the Australian desert – to successfully practise shamanism? My experience after teaching for more than twenty years is that the ability to practise shamanism, including shamanic healing and divination, is an ability that all humans are born with, much as the ability to speak or stand upright. Arvick in this book is clearly a case in point.

But while we are all born with this ability, it is the culture we are born into which defines shamanism. Until recently, there was no definition for shamanism within our culture, and many people who had experiences of shamanic reality either kept quiet about it, not knowing what to do with it, or else were judged by themselves and others to be mentally ill.

Fortunately, this is changing now. More and more, people in western societies are recognising their abilities, as Arvick has done, and are learning with the help of teachers, both in the physical world and the world of the Spirits, how to use this power for their own benefit and for the benefit of others. Also the practice of shamanism is becoming more and more accepted, and shamanic healing is becoming recognised as an alternative method of healing producing positive results.

I am sure Arvick's experiences will seem familiar to many who read this book, and I welcome it as a fine addition to the shamanic literature.

Jonathan Horwitz

Scandinavian Center for Shamanic Studies Copenhagen, Denmark

Alice laughed. 'There's no use trying,' she said; 'one cannot believe impossible things.'

'I daresay you haven't had much practice,' said the Queen. 'When I was your age, I always did it for half an hour a day. Why, sometimes I've believed as many as six impossible things before breakfast.'

Lewis Carroll

Through the Looking Glass

Introduction

It was at my darkest hour that shamanism came into my life. Throughout the years I had experienced many ups and downs and looking back, I can see how the crises of my life always brought me to connect with my power and the potentials which lay hidden within me. The crisis which directed me to my shamanic path was by far the most painful and challenging, yet the fruits it bore were equally as sweet.

I am Armenian, born in Iran, yet have lived most of my adult life in Europe. I started my professional life as a midwife, but eventually came to be a social worker and chose to specialise in the field of child sexual abuse. My work with traumatised children and adult survivors led me to different therapeutic techniques, in search of more ways of reaching and helping them. My search not only led me to different therapies but also took me to different countries. However, at the time, my attention was focused exclusively upon what we may call 'traditional' therapies. It was a health crisis in my life that finally diverted my gaze to alternative options of therapy as well. I was diagnosed as having a degenerative disease of the spine and was told by my doctors that I would end up in a wheelchair. During my stay in New York in the late eighties, I came across Reiki – a spiritual practice and an age-old system of hands-on healing – and decided to learn the method. When Reiki healed my spine disease it also opened my horizons to other possibilities of healing. However, it would still be some time until shamanism came to my life.

After a year of working in New York, I was offered a job in Arizona and moved there. It was there that I became acquainted with The Personal Totem Pole work of Dr E. Stephen Gallegos. I next moved to New Zealand where I was introduced to breath integration. Shamanism was still a long way away. It was only in 1997, following a somewhat strange chain of events, that I found myself on a shamanic course for beginners, conducted by Jonathan Horwitz, who was to become my teacher in ordinary reality. It is not only to my spirit teachers that I owe my gratitude, but also to Jonathan who, hand in hand with them, patiently and lovingly supported me, as I climbed out of the dark hole in which I was at the time.

It was on this first shamanic workshop, that I was told by my spirit helpers I had to write about shamanism. I did not pay attention to the message, since it didn't make sense to me. Why would I write about shamanism? I did not know anything about it. The fact was that the whole experience on the course was strange for me. I felt embarrassed and self-conscious during the rattling rituals and the messages I received on the journeys, as powerful as they were, did not impact on me in any way.

I continued my path with shamanism, however. A few years after that first introductory workshop I stumbled across my course notebook, containing my journeys. As I read through them, I also came across the journey instructing me to write about shamanism. This time, I decided to listen. Although my teachers were not specific in their instructions, I interpreted the message to mean that I had to write a Ph.D. on the subject. When I discussed my realisation with Jonathan, he questioned, in his own quiet way, if I had really understood the message given to me. I was deaf to my teacher's quiet advice and shortly began writing my thesis. I spent many years researching the subject alongside my practice of it. After some time, however, the penny dropped. I realised that I was not intended to write a Ph.D., but rather a book. My

Ph.D. tutor concurred with my decision to abandon the work on my thesis and commence writing a book in its stead.

Alongside the research, my practice of shamanism grew and developed. I gradually integrated shamanic practices into my therapeutic work with people. Throughout the years I have worked with shamanism in many different countries, with many people from all walks of life. I have witnessed people as young as 4 and as old as 75 transform and grow from their encounter with shamanism. I watched with wonder the almost miraculous results of this work and came to realise that it was by far the most powerful therapeutic and spiritual tool I had ever come across.

Shamanism is humanity's oldest healing and spiritual practice. Although, as our world started and continued to modernise, shamanic practices began to fade away, they have been resurrected in recent decades. The first mentions of shamanism were made by anthropologists who travelled far to research the strange customs of foreign tribes around the world. More recently, however, shamanism has reclaimed its place in the western world as a spiritual and therapeutic practice.

This is not an ethnographic study about shamanism, but neither is it a how-to-do instruction book. The heart of the book is centred on the uses of shamanic practices as an empowering tool. By exploring issues of health and healing from a cross-cultural perspective, discussing the nature of spirits and spirituality and looking into other principles of shamanic practices throughout the world, the magic of shamanic journeying is explored and revealed. The book also explores modern or contemporary forms of shamanism, and in particular Core Shamanism and the practice of shamanic counselling, while demonstrating the effectiveness of shamanic journeys to facilitate healing of both psychological and physical problems.

This book was not written by one person. It was co-written and coloured by the words of the spirit teachers as well as those of the many people I have worked with throughout the years, and whose lives and souls were deeply touched and changed by shamanism. On one of my journeys I consulted the spirits on the writing of this book. My guardian spirit told me: 'Let the people tell you. Let the people talk, from their heart. Let them tell you how we have helped them. You are just a channel. Let them write the book, Arvick. That is where its colour and noise will come from. That is how the impossible will be demonstrated.'

Woven throughout the pages of this book are not only the voices of my spirit teachers and people I have worked with, but also the voices of different theoretical approaches. As the book gradually evolved it became apparent to me that my aim in writing it was not to take one single approach to the exploration of shamanism, but rather to integrate different theoretical and philosophical approaches to this ancient spiritual practice. Alongside traditional anthropological knowledge, the wisdom of modern experiential shamanism as well as various psychological theories is intertwined in an attempt to better understand this complex phenomenon.

Throughout the years I have worked with many people. The stories and cases introduced throughout the book are merely the tip of the iceberg. Many stories, just as powerful as the ones presented here, unfortunately remain untold. This book also touches upon my own personal and professional journey to shamanism, as I weave my own life story throughout its chapters. My mother once told me that all people are healers deep down within their soul. 'The healer is in all of us,' she would say, 'and if it is to manifest itself in you in this lifetime, it will come to you when you are ready.' This book is about my own life journey, my journey to shamanism and the journeys of many others, but above all it is the story of the shamanic journey and its power to heal.

Arvick Baghramian

1 Shamanism: Basic Definitions

It is only with the heart that one can see rightly;
What is essential is invisible to the eye.
Antoine de Saint-Exupery, The Little Prince

When I first sat down to write this book, I felt a sudden overwhelming rush that I had so much to say, and didn't know where to start. My head felt like a cauldron full of magic and miracles, all enmeshed and mixed up, bubbling together. The people I had worked with over the years, my own life, the healings and the changes and all the other magical transformations that I had witnessed in myself and in others – all came rushing through. I felt a strong sense of responsibility to the practice, to the people who had allowed me to bring their experiences into this book, to share with the world.

I questioned my ability – would I be able to do this practice the justice it deserved, to project it accurately on paper and paint the full picture? Would I be able to convey to the world the way it felt in my heart, the deep understanding and conviction that I had come to have in this practice, as a result of my own personal experiences, as well as of the powerful healing experiences of others?

To put my thoughts in order, I decided to begin this book with the journey of my own life – and my life journey to shamanism. As I was thinking about this, I saw a flowing river, coursing through valleys, plains, mountains and ravines. I could also see the symbolic connection of this image to my own life. The river of my life had also taken its own course through different landscapes: some smooth and beautiful; others difficult and challenging.

My mother had been a healer and a shaman. The first memory I have of her healing powers dates back to when I was 6 years old. She had been very sick, suffering from extreme abdominal pains, due to post-surgical complications. Throughout her life, my mother had undergone several abdominal operations. During the last of these operations, the surgeon had left a bundle of stitching thread inside her abdomen by mistake.

This had developed into an internal inflammation, causing my mother severe abdominal pains and restricting her ability to move about with ease. Her doctor had diagnosed the problem and had advised her to undergo further surgery. My mother had refused the doctor's advice, saying, 'I will not go under the knife again.' When she left the hospital, she went home and started to treat herself, applying poultices to the inflamed area of her abdomen. As the days went by, her pain worsened, to the point where she could hardly walk or move at all. She steadfastly refused to undergo surgery, however, and continued to treat herself instead.

Six months after beginning her own course of treatment, my mother woke up suddenly at two in the morning, to realise that not only could she move about with ease, but that she could also do so without any pain.

She immediately woke me with the good news. Together, we went to the kitchen, lit the oil lamp, and in the flickering light of the dead of night, carefully unwound the poultices that had been wrapped around her abdomen. Laying on them was the yellowed two-inch long bundle of surgical thread.

My mother and I danced and cried with joy. The miracle had happened! I had naturally also been profoundly affected by my mother's sickness, so the news came as a true miracle to me.

Days later, she shared the information of her healing with her doctor. He also perceived it as being a miracle. I remember being very proud of my mother. That my mum had magic in her hands.

As I grew up, I began to realise that this healing was not a one-off incident. I began to understand that my mother was, in fact, a healer and that she helped heal others as well. In addition to being familiar with the use of medicinal herbs, she was able to mend broken bones, and was also a real wizard with poultices. Unfortunately, I don't recall many of my mother's remedies, but the ones I do, I have been able to use to great effectiveness throughout my life. My mother also had an understanding of the healing powers of colours and successfully used them to alleviate fever, pain and emotional problems.

Up until now, according to current shamanic literature, my mother's knowledge and healing practices would not define her as a shaman, but another aspect of her work would. The reason I have come to understand that my mother was also a shaman was that, during one of the shamanic courses that I attended, I told my teacher, Jonathan Horwitz, that my mother used to be a healer and had helped people in various ways, and that one of her healing practices had been to dream for people. People would come to my mother with their problems and she would dream for them in relation to their problem. 'But Arvick,' Jonathan said, 'Your mother was a shaman.' At the time, Jonathan's statement did not make sense to me. But later as I deepened my studies in shamanism, I came to understand what he meant.

ORIGINS OF SHAMANISM

Shamanism is humanity's oldest spiritual practice and healing profession. Its ancient roots stretch way back in human history, with archaeological findings dating back to Palaeolithic times. Animal skulls and bones found in Europe, dating as far back as 30,000 to 50,000 BC, are believed to have been used for shamanic rituals. More indications of shamanic practices are found in the drawings discovered in the Lascaux caves in France, as well as the Altamira cave in Spain, dating back to around 15,000 BC.[1] Even older testimony to the existence of shamanic practices has been found in the Chauvet cave in France: the impressive and varied animal drawings discovered on the cave walls are thought to be more than 32,000 years old.[2] However, it is impossible to determine how ancient the origins of shamanic practices are. The religious historian Mircea Eliade claims that it is even possible that shamanic practices existed during the hundreds of thousands of years preceding the Stone Age. Indeed, there is no proof to the contrary.[3]

The actual word 'shaman' first appeared in 1672 in the memoirs of exiled Russian churchman Avvakum, and later in the writings of Dutchman Nicholas Witsen. It is through Witsen's writings that the term was first introduced to western scholars. Mircea Eliade, in his comprehensive work, *Shamanism: Archaic Techniques of Ecstasy,*[4] refers to the Tungus tribes of Siberia as the source for the term 'shaman', pronounced by them as 'sˇaman'. Two different meanings to the word have been suggested: one, proposed by I.M. Lewis,[5] is 'one who is excited, moved, or raised', the other, by Diózegi[6] is 'the one who knows', coming from the root 'sa', meaning 'to know'. Halifax[7] claims that the term shaman may have originated from the Vedic *sram,* meaning 'to heat oneself or practice austerities'. In other cultures around the world, some of the different meanings of the word shaman are 'the one who sees in the dark' and 'the one who drops to the bottom of the sea'.

However, although the actual word 'shaman' has now come to be used as a blanket term to refer to all 'shamanic' practitioners around the world, it is important to acknowledge that it is a specific term belonging to only one specific culture. According to Hutton,[8] the term 'shaman' is 'a crude and convenient piece of European labelling'. He claims the word was adopted for use by the first Dutch researchers who came to Siberia, due to the simple fact that it was easy for them to pronounce it. The fact is, however, that not only do shamanic societies around the world use completely different words when referring to their 'shaman' (for example, the Jivaro use the word *'Uwis͞in'*, the Tapirapé *'Panche'*, the Piaroa *'Ruwang'* and the Inuit *'Angaqoq'*), but within Siberia itself, the word 'shaman' is not used among the majority of its aboriginal inhabitants. For example, the Yakuts use *'Oyuna'*, the Samoyedic-speakers, *'Tadibey'* and the Turkic-speaking people use the term *'Kam'* when referring to their shaman.[9]

Unlike the term 'shaman', 'shamanism' is a theoretical concept, created by scholars and used to group together beliefs and practices from all around the world which have a clear association to those existing in Siberia. Shamanism is a worldwide phenomenon. Strikingly similar shamanic beliefs and practices have been observed in different cultures around the world.

Eliade[10] reviewed a vast anthropological literature on the subject in an attempt to establish one general definition of shamanism. He noted that many different titles were given to shamans, such as 'magician', 'sorcerer', 'physician', 'priest' or 'political leader'. He thus stressed the importance of distinguishing the shaman from other practitioners of magic, religion or healing. The shaman, according to Eliade, is a magician, but not all magicians are shamans. The shaman is a medicine man, but not all medicine men are shamans. The shaman, unlike the magician or the sorcerer, uses a technique that is unique to him or her – ecstasy, or a shifting of consciousness into an altered state. Shamans are the masters of ecstasy, according to Eliade, but it is not the practice of ecstasy alone that defines them. Not every ecstatic could be considered a shaman. The shaman's ecstasy is specific – he or she 'specialises in a trance during which his soul is believed to leave his body and ascend to the sky or descend to the underworld'.[11]

In the last half of the twentieth century, shamanism was reintroduced to the West, in the form of a therapeutic or 'self-help' practice. This can be credited to Michael Harner,[12] the first person to bring shamanism out of the academic and anthropological world and into the practical sphere of therapy and healing in the West. Harner, an anthropologist who studied for many years with both South and North American shamans, reintroduced shamanic practices to the West under the title of 'Core Shamanism'. He provides his own definition of a shaman (and thus of shamanism): 'A man or woman who enters an altered state of consciousness – at will – to contact and utilize an ordinarily hidden reality in order to acquire knowledge, power, and to help other persons. The shaman has at least one, and usually more, "spirits" in his personal service'. Unlike Eliade's definition, which is centred on the practice of ecstasy and travel to the sky or the underworld, Harner's definition also clarifies the purpose for which the shaman journeys to these realms – 'to acquire knowledge, power, and to help other persons'.

In modern shamanic practices, the process of journeying typically begins with setting a mission or question, stating the purpose for which the shaman wishes to contact the spirits. This is followed by darkening the surroundings, lying down and covering the eyes. Using the sound of the drum, the shaman goes into an altered state of consciousness. This shifting of consciousness is what we refer to as 'journeying'.

During the journey, the shaman receives the answers and messages relevant to their mission from their spirit helpers and teachers. These messages are communicated to them in the form of images, words, sounds or experiences. At the end of the journey, again by the help of the drum, the shaman shifts their consciousness back to its ordinary state and return from the journey with the messages given to them.

The reintroduction of shamanism into the western world has resulted in the emergence of a new type of shaman – the shamanic counsellor, or modern shaman. Shamanic practices are now used by many in the West as a spiritual path or a form of therapeutic tool, and while many engage in shamanic practices solely for their own personal growth, others have chosen to take on the ancient role of the shaman, to support others to come into contact with the spirit world as well. I believe that shamanic counsellors or contemporary shamans perform a role which is essentially similar to that of the ancient shamans, but with one crucial difference – the shamanic counsellor is not responsible for the well-being of an organised community. Their responsibility is solely to the people who come to them in search of help. Still, both ancient and modern shamans share the same responsibility towards those who seek them.

Finally, we must address an important question relating to the origins of shamanic practices: how is it, some ask, that different societies, separated by time, space and language, are found to have so much in common when it comes to shamanism? The widespread speculation suggests the possibility of prehistoric contact between the people of different regions due to migration. It is through this contact, many claim, that shamanic practices have spread all over the world. A different view, however, is proposed by Michael Harner.[13]

How is it, Harner asks, that only these particular practices should be passed down for more than 20,000 years, while other social aspects are found to be in great contrast between these very same cultures? He suggests that the prevalence of shamanic techniques around the globe is in fact a testimony to their effectiveness and that it is through a process of trial and error that the same healing techniques were created and adopted by different societies. In other words, Harner claims that shamanism developed in a parallel fashion throughout the world, pointing to a possible evolutionary process of human consciousness, shaped by common social factors and innate tendencies. It is this evolutionary process which inspired the collective expression of shamanism into being, rather than migratory factors, according to Harner.

SHAMANISM AND RELIGION

The question whether or not shamanism is a religion or religious phenomenon is an old one. Throughout the years, scholars and writers have provided many conflicting views and opinions on the matter, and, to date, there is far from a consensus on this issue. Part of the problem in deciding whether or not shamanism is a religion lies in the difficulty of actually defining shamanism and defining religion. Many attempts have been made to provide coherent definitions for both phenomena, and in both cases no one agreed-upon definition has been reached. Thus, I believe that a consensual answer to the question will probably never be reached.

Although we cannot assert, then, that shamanism is not a religion, it is certainly clear that shamanism does not 'look' like a religion: it is free of any sets of doctrines or religious dogmas; it is not based upon a hierarchy of power; there are no specific buildings designed for worship; and nor are any acts of worship *per se* involved in shamanic practice. However, shamanism does impart a belief in the existence of the supernatural world, the spirits, and a faith in the shaman's ability to contact them. For some, these facts alone would be sufficient to define shamanism as a religion or as fulfilling a religious role.

Still, it is interesting to note that all definitions of shamanism are focused on practices, rather than upon the existence of certain belief systems – the shaman is defined by their actions rather than by what they believe in. Harner[14] claims that 'shamanism ultimately is only a method, not a religion with a fixed set of dogmas'. Eliade[15] also states that, in fact, 'Shamanism is not a religion *per se*, but a system of ecstatic and therapeutic methods whose purpose is to obtain contact with the parallel, yet invisible, universe of the spirits and win its support in dealing with human affairs.'

Following my own experience with shamanic practices, I consider shamanism to be a *spiritual practice* rather than a religion. I find that the effectiveness of shamanic journeys is not dependent on one's belief system and thus, that it is not necessary to worship, or, in fact, even to believe in the existence of, spirits, in order for the journey to take its effect.

For example, some people I have worked with referred to spirits as either archetypes or believed that they were a figment of their imagination. The transformation within them following the shamanic work, however, still took place. Throughout my travels, I have also worked with people from different religious backgrounds and found that the difference in religious beliefs had no effect on the quality, nature and effectiveness of their journeys. Even religious-orthodox people had no difficulties journeying, and neither did they perceive shamanic practice to interfere with their religious beliefs.

In conclusion, I believe that shamanism can better be understood as a way of seeing the world, and find that the term 'religion' is in many ways an impediment to the comprehension of the shamanic worldview, be it indigenous or modern. I have found an echo of my experience in Harner's[16] words: 'The ancient way is powerful, and taps so deeply into the human mind, that one's usual cultural belief systems and assumptions about reality are essentially irrelevant.'

THE SHAMAN AND THE SPIRITS

Another important element in the definition of shamanism concerns the relationship of the shaman with their spirits. Eliade[17] describes this relationship as one of 'mastery', where the shaman is not controlled or 'possessed' by the spirits, but rather, is in control of them. Other researchers of classic shamanism hold a similar view on the matter and refer to the shaman as controlling their spirits or even owning a crew of them. The issue of the shaman's control over their helping spirits is an even more central component in both Shirokogoroff's[18] and I.M. Lewis's[19] definitions, in comparison to Eliade's.

However, even in the classic literature about shamanism we come across many accounts depicting a different relationship between the shaman and their spirit helpers; a relationship in which the shaman does not control the spirits, but rather begs and implores them for help. Hutton actually cites examples of shamans cajoling and persuading spirits for help among the Tungusic-speaking tribes in Siberia (which was the area in which Shirokogoroff conducted his research).[20]

Jonathan Horwitz is my shamanic teacher in ordinary reality. An anthropologist by training, and a former student and colleague of Michael Harner, Jonathan has been teaching shamanism in the form of self-help courses in Europe for the past 19 years. His definition of shamanism differs from that of Eliade and Shirokogoroff on the subject of control. In his own words:

A shaman is someone who changes his or her state of consciousness at will, in order to journey to another reality, 'a non-ordinary reality', the world of the spirits, where she meets with her spirit helpers to ask for help, power, or knowledge for herself and/or others. Mission accomplished, the shaman journeys back to ordinary reality where she uses or dispenses the newly gained knowledge and/or power.[21]

Here, the relationship of the shaman with the spirits is not one of mastery and control, but rather a relationship in which the shaman is a recipient of help, knowledge and power.

It seems that there are many different views regarding the nature of the shaman's relationship with their spirits. I believe that this is a testimony to the complexity of the shamanic phenomenon and that every academic or practitioner in this field has formed their definition based on their own experience and encounters with it.

However, we must also consider the possibility that the debate regarding control also has something to do with mere terminology. It is possible that in using the word 'control' anthropologists and scholars were merely trying to clarify that unlike other magic-religious practitioners, shamans were not controlled or possessed by their spirit allies, but rather addressed them and communicated with them *at will*. This is possible especially in the light of Eliade's[22] assertion regarding the importance of differentiating between shamanism and cases of spirit possession.

Even as a beginner in this field, when I first came across definitions claiming mastery of the shaman over their helping spirits, I was baffled. Never in my experience and encounters with my spirit helpers had I ever perceived myself as controlling or mastering them. For me, the word 'control' denotes the use of manipulative power, and I believe that the need or will to control others arises from an experience of fear or helplessness.

Throughout the years of my work in this field I have come to develop a high regard and a trusting relationship with my spirit helpers. I thus do not have, and never have had, any fear of being controlled by them. I recognise, however, that there is an element of control involved in shamanic journeying– that being a measure of mastery over the *self*. The shaman is a bridge between two worlds – with one foot in the world of the spirits and the other in the world of ordinary reality. In order to journey effectively they must maintain their balance between these two worlds, and to do that shamans must have a measure of control over their own state of consciousness.

While journeying, I retain an awareness of the purpose of my journey at all times, with one foot remaining in the ordinary world. On the other hand, I let go of my mind in order to be able to hear the spirits, without allowing my own thoughts and preconceptions to influence and contaminate the teachings I am receiving – with the other foot in the world of the spirits.

In one of my journeys I asked my guardian spirit to explain the issue of control. This was his answer to me:

'Think about the word control, Arvick. You have a choice to stop now and leave me. How am I controlling you? And if I wanted to, I could just disappear. How are you controlling me? It's a mutual decision. You decide to come and we decide to teach. You choose to let go and allow us to help you, to offer you the keys that open the doors, where you can see beyond.'

THE SHAMAN'S UNIVERSE

To fully understand the role of the shaman, one must first understand the principles that form the shaman's world. Three basic principles or beliefs could be regarded as common to all shamanic societies: firstly, the basic belief in the existence of spirits and spirit worlds, where knowledge, power and healing is found. Secondly, the belief that the universe is comprised of three cosmic zones, connected together by a central axis. And thirdly, a belief in animism, or in other words, the belief that everything, including seemingly inanimate objects, possesses a soul or spirit.

In many shamanic societies, shamans occupy multiple roles and positions. The shaman is a doctor, psychologist, pharmacist, poet, dancer, philosopher, storyteller, sociologist and priest– encompassing the different roles which have split into different professions in our western world.[23] The shaman may function as a village leader, engages in economic and political activities and conducts religious ceremonies. However, the most important aspect in the work of the shaman is, without doubt, their ability to mediate between the invisible world of the spirits, and the material world of our daily existence. Symbolically, as was mentioned before, the shaman could be seen to have one foot in the spirit world, and the other in the material one.

For indigenous cultures that practise shamanism, the spirit world is as real as the material world. It is the place where spirits reside, and thus it is the place from where knowledge, power and help can be brought back. For some, like the Jivaro, it is the invisible world of the spirits which is the true world, while the ordinary material reality is nothing but a lie, a deception or an illusion. Such a worldview creates an understandable need for shamans – individuals who have the ability to cross over and journey to the real world of the spirits in order to retrieve from there the knowledge, power and healing needed for their people.

The realm of the spirits is divided into three cosmic regions– the sky, the earth and the underworld, or the upper, middle, and lower worlds, with all three connected by a central axis. At the heart of shamanic practice lies the journey to the spirit world, the crossing from one cosmic region to another, and it is the shaman who is able to traverse these regions at will, for it is the shaman who is familiar with the structure of the universe.

Contact and communication with the spirits is facilitated mostly though an alteration in the shaman's state of consciousness. Different titles have been given to describe the state of consciousness which characterises the shamanic journey. Carlos Castaneda,[24] in his stories of the teachings of the Yaqui shaman Don Juan, provides a clear distinction between two different types of consciousness or realities: the ordinary and non-ordinary reality. The shamanic journey is carried out in non-ordinary reality. Harner[25] refers to the state of consciousness which characterises our normal waking life as an 'ordinary state of consciousness (OSC)' and to that which characterises the shaman's journey the 'shamanic state of consciousness (SSC)'. As noted before, Eliade refers to the state of consciousness characterising the shamanic journey as a state of 'ecstasy'. In this case, however, 'ecstasy' does not refer so much to a sensation of bliss or nirvana, but to a sensation of moving out of one's normal state of consciousness, or transcending the boundaries of the ego.

Different methods of inducing this state are found among different cultures. Hallucinogenic drugs, large amounts of alcohol, tobacco leaves used in a variety of forms, singing, dancing, blinking and even yawning – all have been, and still are, used as tools or aids to reach a shamanic state of consciousness. There is no doubt, however, that the drum and rattle are by far the most important vehicles of transportation to the non-ordinary reality which the shaman possesses. Used by shamans in virtually every society around the world, the drum has been referred to as 'the shaman's canoe' or 'the shaman's horse'. In more modern terminology, we could even refer to it as 'the shaman's Rolls-Royce'.

In some societies, another way of entering the spirit world is through dreaming. The Tapirapé, for example, believe that while dreaming the soul of the person frees itself from the body and moves freely in the realm of the supernatural world.[26] In fact, certain tribes, like those of North Western Australia, use the actual word 'dreaming' when referring to the shamanic journey. The Jivaro believe that only in dreams does true reality reveal itself to man. They differentiate between two different types of dreams: 'normal dreams', which come through natural sleep, and the dream which is produced by artificial means. They consider both types to hold vital and important information, yet the dreams which are considered to be the most prophetic in nature are those that have been produced by ingesting *natemä** and tobacco water. Receiving messages from the spirits while in this state of induced sleep is referred to by the Jivaro as *wuimektinyu,* meaning 'to see'.[27]

Another belief shared by different shamanic societies around the world is that everything is alive. For the shaman, objects, plants, animals and the universe itself all possess a living spirit or soul. This notion of an animistic world is vividly expressed in the words of a Chukchi shaman:

All that exists lives. The lamp walks around. The walls of the houses have voices of their own. Even the chamber-vessel has a separate land and house. The skins sleeping in the bags talk at night. The antlers lying on the tombs arise at night and walk in procession around the mounds, while the deceased get up and visit the living.[28]

Through shamanic practice we can all come into direct contact with the spirits of nature in search for help and wisdom. This is beautifully demonstrated by a story told to me by one of the people who participated in one of my courses about an experience he had while talking to the spirit of a tree.

---

* Natemä is a hallucinogenic drink used by shamans to enter an altered state of consciousness. This brew is prepared from segments of two kinds of vines and has a chemical structure similar to that of LSD.

Being a university professor, he was invited by a friend and colleague from the USA to co-write a paper. He gladly embarked on this project, only later to encounter great difficulties in working with his colleague. Just as he was about to give up on the project and return to Israel, he remembered his experience from one of my courses of talking to the spirit of a rock. As he was wandering in the gardens of the university, a willow tree caught his attention. He went over to the tree, asking its spirit to advise him how to deal with his problem.

The answers he received were surprising to him, yet extremely helpful. Following the advice he had received from the spirit of the tree he was able to successfully finish co-writing the paper, as well as save his friendship with his colleague in the process.

The notion of animism is not foreign to me. It takes me back to the times I witnessed my mother talking to the mountain, asking for strength, and for the waters of the spring at the bottom of it to take her sadness away. 'I give you my pain for you to take away with you,' she used to say. Every morning she would sing to the birds, asking them to take messages to her brothers in Armenia.

When I think of the world around me as alive, I am also reminded that help, power and knowledge is always available, that it is literally all around us, that it can be found in the simplest of things and in the most unexpected of places.

* * *

The journey that I have undertaken to study, work with and understand shamanism has also been a healing journey for me

The 6-year-old child, who was affected by the sickness and suffering of her mother, welcomed the miracle of her mother's recovery and was proud of her. As I grew older, however, I became increasingly aware of my mother's differentness. Except for the healing I talked about at the beginning of this chapter, I never appreciated my mother's knowledge. I was embarrassed by it. 'Don't do it in front of my friends,' I used to tell her. She was known as 'the woman who helped people', and was respected by all. But with that came the edge of being different. And I felt that.

Later on in my life, as I came to work with shamanism and read about it, I found myself feeling familiar with the information in many of the books I came across. I felt I was at home reading about all of these things. It took me back to my culture and to my home, my life as a child. Only reading about it in books gave 'credibility' to my childhood experiences. In a way, it was healing the shame that I had felt, taking away the judgment I had about my mother's healing work and putting it in a positive light. Reading about shamanism in books, I also came to feel sadness and regret for not having appreciated what my mother had been doing. Almost all children go through a process of being embarrassed by their parents, and later on, it either does or does not affect their lives. Today I am proud of my mother; my embarrassment about her has been healed. Shamanism has helped me to understand and appreciate who my mother was. And so my journey into shamanism has been, for me, not only a journey of healing, but a journey back to myself.

2 The Shaman's Dream: Calling and Initiation

> Behold, a sacred voice is calling you;
> All over the sky a sacred voice is calling.
> From the initiatory experience of Black Elk,

As far back as my memory can go, I remember my mother telling me, 'You are a very special baby. You are a miracle baby. Only one in a hundred survives.' And then she would tell me how desperately she wanted a baby, and how happy she was when she first learned she was pregnant with me. She was in her early forties when she discovered that she was pregnant, and her pregnancy was not an ordinary one. I was not in her uterus, but in her abdomen – an abdominal pregnancy.

The night of my birth, my mother did not suffer contractions. Instead, she developed an unusually painful toothache. It was a very stormy night and she was rushed to the hospital in an open carriage. By midday the doctors performed an abdominal section. I was born. I was alive.

Death was present in my life since the moment of my birth, or rather, my conception. Only one out of a hundred abdominal pregnancy babies actually survives, and against all odds I was one of them. The next time I confronted death was in my early teens, when I nearly died of severe food poisoning. My mother would always have a dish of dates in my room, and I would eat them as I studied. One particular time the dates had apparently been contaminated by a poisonous lizard that walked on them. Very shortly after eating the dates I began vomiting and had diarrhoea. By the time I was *brought to the hospital I was completely dehydrated. The doctors thought I was dying. My mother was by my side, forcing me to slowly drink special herb teas that she had brewed, but the prognosis was grim. When my condition started to gradually improve the doctors were shocked. It took me a full month to recover. I had to remain at all times in an air conditioned room and could not eat anything solid. But I had miraculously survived. A second time.*

The next crisis in my life came when I was 16. I had fallen deeply in love with my private English teacher. He was a man older than me and had encouraged me at first. However, eventually he seemed to have realised how improper our relationship would be. He harshly rejected me and left his position. The shock of the experience sent me into a state of deep depression. All I can remember of those days was lying on the bed, crying and talking to myself. People around me couldn't make sense of what I was saying, and didn't know what to do. I stayed like that for a while, until finally, following the doctor's advice, I was put on Librium. This, apparently, worsened my condition, and I began to have hallucinations, mumbling incoherently most of the time. I was living in a dream world. My mother decided to take drastic action. She took me away from where we were living and travelled with me back to Isfahan – my birth place. We stayed there for a while. She took me off the Librium and started treating me with herbal teas and infusions. She dreamed for me, and took me out to nature. After a month I gradually recovered, until finally I was myself again.

THE CALL TO BECOME A SHAMAN

In cultures where shamanism is practised, the potential shaman undergoes an initiatory period during which they are instructed in the arts of healing, and acquire the tools necessary for their vocation. As a rule, it is quite rare for shamans to be called to their vocation past a certain age. Evidence from numerous cultures indicates that shamans are summoned most often during childhood, adolescence or early adulthood. In some cases, the shaman-to-be would be chosen even prior to, or immediately after, their birth. Among the Chukchi tribe of Siberia, for example, it was extremely rare for a future shaman to be called by the spirits past the age of 40, while in the case of the Coyotes, another Siberian tribe, girls would receive the call between the ages of 10 and 12, and boys between the ages of 20 and 25.[1] Similarly, among the South American Piaroa tribe, the education of shamans begins at the age of 12 or 13.[2]

The answers to the question 'who becomes a shaman?' are many, and depend on the specific culture we examine. Some generalisations, however, can be made. Both men and women can be chosen to become shamans. In some cultures, men would be chosen more frequently than women, in others, women would be favoured to men, while in yet others no clear distinction can be made. However, one element that can be found in all shamanic societies is that *shamans are chosen to their vocation*, rather than choose it themselves. It takes the call and approval of the spirits to make a shaman.

The spirits' indication that a person has been chosen to become a shaman takes different forms in different cultures. The shaman-to-be may have unusual experiences or exhibit strange behaviours, be afflicted with a certain illness such as epilepsy, possess unusual physical features, or recover unexpectedly from severe or prolonged sickness. Nahoum Megged[3] tells of the shaman Don Lucio, who was struck by lightning and spent three years in a coma before waking up and beginning to practise shamanism. As a result of his unusual experience he had become a 'weather shaman' and was believed to be able to control or influence the weather.

The call to shamanism may also come in the form of a special dream. Henry Rupert, a Washo shaman of North America, was called to shamanise through a dream he had when he was 17. In his dream he saw a horned buck standing in the west and facing east. He then heard a voice telling him: 'don't kill my babies any more', and woke up to discover that he was bleeding from his nose. When he looked outside his window he saw that it was raining. Henry understood his dream to be a power dream, which not only directed him towards shamanhood, but also conferred certain powers upon him. He interpreted his dream to mean that the conjunction of the buck (known as the 'boss of the rain') and the rain outside his window implied that he could control the weather. The presence of the rain also indicated to him that water would be his main spiritual guide while the nosebleed was taken to be a sign that his dream had been indeed a message from the spirits and not just an ordinary dream.[4]

Dreams in general play a very important role in many shamanic societies. They are considered to be messages from the spirits, are likened to shamanic journeying and thus are taken seriously. The information that may be acquired in the dream is just as powerful and meaningful as information acquired on a shamanic journey. The only difference is that while the shamanic journey is taken at will, dreams come involuntarily. Among the Tapirapé, one of the early signs of becoming a *panché* (shaman), is a childhood inclination to dream. As Wagley[5] reports:

[I was] told . . . that one young boy, an orphan and therefore badly cared for, would certainly make a powerful shaman. This boy turned and talked in his sleep and had been known to cry during a nightmare. He remembered few of his dreams but spoke of seeing the spirit of his mother; he also described an evil spirit which he met during a dream. One of the then living powerful shamans also had had a predilection for dreaming as a youngster.

The shamanic initiation call might also come during a 'vision quest'. This is a period during which the aspiring shaman goes into isolation and fasting in order to contact the spirits. While in isolation, the future shaman may perform certain rituals and attempt to avoid sleep. The purpose of the vision quest is making a first contact with one's spirits, or gain the ability to see spirits. If the person manages to see visions and have experiences of encountering spirits, that would confirm that they have the magical powers necessary to become a shaman.

Igjugarjuk, a Caribou Eskimo shaman, told Knud Rasmussen[6] of his quest for 'spirit vision':

When I was to be a shaman, I chose suffering through the two things that were most dangerous to us humans, suffering through hunger and suffering through cold . . . My instructor was my wife's father, Perqánâq. When I was to be exhibited to Pinga and Hila, he dragged me on a little sledge that was not bigger than I could just sit on it; he dragged me far . . . it was in winter time and took place at night with the new moon . .

. I was not fetched again until the next moon was of the same size . . . Perqánâq built a small snow hut at the place where I was to be, this snow hut being no bigger than that I could just get under cover and sit down. I was given no sleeping skin to protect me against the cold, only a little piece of Caribou skin to sit upon . . . the entrance was closed with a block, but no soft snow was thrown over the hut to make it warm. When I had sat there five days, Perqánâq came with water . . . Not until fifteen days afterwards did he come again and hand me the same . . . and then he was gone again, for even the old shaman must not interrupt my solitude . . . As soon as I had become alone, Perqánâq enjoined me to think of one single thing all the time I was to be there, to want only one single thing, and that was to draw Pinga's attention to the fact that there I sat and wished to be a shaman . . . my novitiate took place in the middle of the coldest winter, and I, who never got anything to warm me, and must not move, was very cold, and it was so tiring having to sit without daring to lie down, that sometimes it was as if I died a little. Only towards the end of the thirty days did a helping spirit come to me, a lovely and beautiful helping spirit, whom I had never thought of; it was a white woman; she came to me whilst I had collapsed, exhausted, and was sleeping. But still I saw her lifelike, hovering over me . . .

Among the Tapirapé, those who were not called to shamanism by a spontaneous dream, would gather on a certain day in the centre of the village to seek dreams. The spirit world would then be accessed by inhaling tobacco smoke; the novice would sit with the practising shaman and swallow smoke from his tutor's pipe until he began to vomit. At this point the shaman would take the pipe from the novice and hold it, forcing him to continue inhaling smoke. This process would continue until the novice became unconscious. It was during this time that the novice might experience the sought-after initiatory dream.[7]

As we have seen, the spirits are the crucial component in the appointing of a new shaman – without the call or approval of the spirits, there is no shaman. Seeing spirits, whether while dreaming or awake, spontaneously or voluntarily, determines the vocation of the future shaman. In some tribes, individuals may appoint themselves to be shamans. However, as a rule, these practitioners are regarded by their community to be less powerful and effective than their 'colleagues' who were chosen for their vocation by the spirits.

Finally, in some cultures heredity also plays a factor in the selection of future shamans. The phenomenon is especially common in Siberia. Hutton[8] notes that most shamans among the Siberian tribes of the south and south-west were the immediate descendants of other practising shamans: 'In some respects', he concludes, 'Siberian shamanism was a craft, and in traditional societies crafts often run in families.' Even in these cases, however, no shaman was chosen to their craft without the explicit call of the spirits.

The spirits' call, however, is not always accepted joyfully, and may be received with ambivalence or even strong refusal. Some cases have been documented in which a young man or woman receiving the call of the spirits attempts at first to refuse the invitation. Such a case was documented by the Russian, Bogoras,[9] who spent many years among the Chukchi of Siberia:

> Young people, as a rule, are exceedingly reluctant to obey the call, especially if it involves the adoption of some characteristic device in clothing or in the mode of life. They refuse to take the drum and to call the 'spirits', leave the amulets in the field out of fear, etc. The parents of young persons 'doomed to inspiration' act differently, according to temperament and family conditions. Sometimes they protest against the call coming to their child, and try to induce it to reject the 'spirits' and to keep to the ordinary life . . .

Among the Sedang Moi, a man called to the spirits might take steps as drastic as drinking his own urine in the hope of losing favour with his spirits, and being relieved of his shamanic duties.[10] Such attempts, however, are more often futile than successful. The repercussions of denying the call of the spirits are believed, among the majority of shamanic societies, to be of the gravest sort, and to result in illness, insanity and even death.

The French anthropologist George Devereux[11] reported of interviewing a man who had been hospitalised at the time of the interview with the diagnosis of manic depressive psychosis. Both the man and his community members insisted that the reason for his illness was his refusal to answer the call of the spirits and to practise shamanism.

As we have seen, there are a variety of ways in which shamans are traditionally called to their vocation. This initial call by the spirits is also considered to be the onset of the shaman's initiation into their new craft.

INITIATION CRISIS

While it is possible for the prospective shaman to dismiss dreams, visions and other significant signs calling them to their vocation, the initiation crisis, which many experience, certainly cannot be ignored. As I have said, in some cases, the shaman is called to their vocation through illness. This can be either psychological or physical illness and cases have been documented of shamans initiated into their profession after having suffered depression, dissociative disorders, psychotic episodes or severe physical diseases such as smallpox. Other unusual symptoms or behaviours such as hypersensitivity and changes in perception have also been reported. At times, the neophyte might even exhibit dangerous, life-threatening behaviours. These experiences can be so dramatic that they have come to be known as the shamanic initiation crisis and can only be relieved once the prospective shaman begins to shamanise.

The famous Yakut shaman, Tüspüt, whose name means 'fallen from the sky', had become ill when he was 20. He reported that he recovered from his illness only after he began to sing (meaning to shamanise). When met by Sieroszewski in his sixties he displayed great health and was full of energy: 'If necessary, he can drum, dance, jump all night'. Throughout his life Tüspüt had travelled a great deal and even worked in the gold mines, but he reported that he would become unwell if he did not practise shamanism for a certain period of time.[12]

A Goldi shaman told of a similar experience: '. . . up to the age of 20 I was quite well. Then I felt ill, my whole body ailed me, I had bad headaches. Shamans tried to cure me, but it was all to no avail. When I began shamaning myself, I got better and better. It is now ten years that I have been a shaman . . .' Finally, an especially unusual and interesting story is that of a Buryat man, who as a youth strongly rejected shamanism. His story began when he became ill and in spite of all efforts, including seeking the help of traditional doctors, could not recover from his illness. He finally resorted to shamanising, and was immediately cured. He then continued practising as a shaman for the rest of his life.[13]

At times the initiation call would not manifest itself in sudden illness but rather in a slow change of the person's behaviour. The shaman-to-be might become meditative, withdraw from the community by either isolating themselves or sleeping for long periods of time, appear absent-minded, have meaningful dreams and in some cases even seizures. These experiences drastically disrupt the life of the shaman-to-be, leading to inner imbalance, and finally bring about the birth of their new 'shaman self'.

DEATH AND REBIRTH

As we have seen, there are many ways in which the shaman may receive their call from the spirits. At times, the initial call, or crisis, whether in the form of illness, dreams or visions, is merely an indication that the person has been chosen by the spirits to become a shaman. However, the initial call usually also constitutes an initiation on its own and has the power to begin the transformation process of the person into a shaman. Initiatory experiences, as a rule, follow the basic structure of an initiation ceremony: suffering, symbolic death and resurrection. From this point of view, a call through illness also functions as an initiatory experience, due to the suffering the shaman-to-be goes through.

Stories of frightening initiations are many. A vivid description given by an Australian shaman of the Yaralde tribe demonstrates the horrors encountered by the neophyte on their initiatory journey to the spirit world:

> When you lie down to see the prescribed visions, and you do see them, do not be frightened . . . You see your camp burning and the blood waters rising, and thunder, lightning and rain, the earth rocking, the hills moving... Do not be frightened. If you get up, you will not see these scenes, but when you lie down again, you will see them, unless you get too frightened. If you do, you will break the web (or thread) on which the scenes are hung. You may see dead persons walking towards you, and you will hear their bones rattle. If you hear and see these things without fear, you will never be frightened of anything . . . you are now powerful because you have seen these dead people.[14]

The recurring experiences reported across cultures are those of death and rebirth, where the neophyte, while in an altered state of consciousness, may undergo physical dismemberment and reconstruction or be reduced into a skeleton. During the initiatory journey of a Yakut shaman, the neophyte has his limbs cut up, his bones cleaned and the flesh scraped off them. His bodily fluids are disposed of and his eyes ripped from their sockets. The bones are then gathered and fastened together with iron. The ceremony, which lasts from three to seven days, takes place in a solitary location, during which the neophyte lies unmoving, and appears to be dead.[15]

Another example is an account given by Popov, telling of an Avam Samoyed (Siberian) shaman. This shaman, who was afflicted with smallpox, appeared to be so sick that he was almost buried while still alive. His initiation took place in the days of his sickness, while unconscious. He recalled being carried to the centre of the sea, where the spirit of the smallpox appeared to him, carrying a message: 'from the Lords of the Water you will receive the gift of shamanising. Your name as a shaman will be *Huottarie* [Diver]'. The shaman neophyte then went on to meet several spirits, and descended to the underworld where he met the spirits of various illnesses, thus acquiring the knowledge of how to cure these same illnesses in ordinary reality. At the end of this journey the shaman's body was dismembered, he was decapitated and his body parts put in a cauldron over a burning fire for three years. The shaman was then fashioned a new head and his bones reassembled. He now possessed new eyes, with which he could gain insight into the spirit world, and new ears to allow him to understand the language of plants. *Huottarie* was now ready to take on the role of a shaman.[16]

Symbolic death can also be experienced by the neophyte through exposure to extreme fatigue, torture, fasting and physical harm during the initiation. A Jivaro neophyte who wishes to become a shaman must go through quite an ordeal in order to attain his first 'spirit vision'. He must fast for days and drink great amounts of tobacco juice. When a spirit finally appears before the neophyte, the master shaman immediately begins to strike him until he falls unconscious to the ground.[17] The pain he experiences after awakening is the proof that a spirit has possessed him. All the suffering, the pain, the intoxications and beatings that have caused him to become unconscious can be equivalent to a ritual death.

The death and rebirth experience is of great importance to the development of the shaman. The initiate must first symbolically die before becoming a shaman. However, instead of true death, this symbolic act grants the shaman great powers. What would kill any other person makes the true shaman invulnerable and powerful, leading them over and beyond the threshold of death. The shaman is not an ordinary person; hence, the ordinary person within them must die before the shaman can be born.

Shamanic cultures are not alone in regarding encounters with death to be potentially transformative. Many religions as well as several modern psychological theories hold a similar view. For 'a confrontation with one's personal death . . . has the power to provide a massive shift in the way one lives in the world... Death acts as a catalyst that can move one from one stage of being to a higher one'.[18] This theme of death–rebirth is weaved throughout the world's cultures, myths, religions and spiritual practices, where the confrontation is not only with a physical death, but also with the death of the ego. This is the process of shedding an old identity that no longer serves us in favour of a new one.

Roger Walsh[19] provides an ancient example to this recurring theme in the words of Jesus:

> Some two thousand years ago Jesus spoke of the importance of this process in a metaphor that has echoed across centuries: 'a grain of wheat remains a solitary grain unless it falls

into the ground and dies; but if it dies, it brings a rich harvest'. The experience of death–rebirth can bring a rich harvest. As with many other psychological and spiritual transformations, it was the shamans who were the first to recognise and harvest it.

ARE SHAMANS MENTALLY ILL?

The psychological health of shamans has been one of the most debated subjects among western scholars and researchers over the years. It has been argued that shamans are psychologically disturbed and, more specifically, that they are in fact schizophrenics. Although more popular in past years than today, this view is still held among some contemporary writers. Two shamanic behaviours in particular have been interpreted by western researchers as pathological. The first is the shamanic journey and the second is the initiation crisis.

The journey contains several characteristics likely to arouse the suspicion of western researchers. The alteration in the state of consciousness, the visions and sensory experiences of the shaman, the acute changes in behaviour and the belief in a communication with supernatural beings – all would seem foreign or strange to contemporary westerners, and so might lead to the conclusion that the shaman is mentally ill. The initial crisis is even more suspicious, with its occasional psychosis-like symptoms, and the acute changes in behaviour which sometimes characterise it.

Richard Noll[20] addresses this issue at length, in his comprehensive paper on the subject. He concludes that the diagnosis of shamans as schizophrenics is born out of a fundamental failure to differentiate between the nature and characteristics of the shamanic state of consciousness as opposed to those of the schizophrenic state of consciousness.

He identifies the most important difference to be that of volition: the shaman is a 'master of ecstasy: wilfully enters and leaves the altered state; the schizophrenic exerts no control over such activity and is the hapless victim of delusion, with a notable impairment in role functioning'.[21] For the shaman to be able to fulfil their role effectively, it is imperative that they maintain a high and respectable status within their community. It is thus essential for them to demonstrate a high measure of self-mastery in both ordinary reality and while journeying to the spirit world. This mastery is derived from the shaman's ability to differentiate between one reality and another – something which is impossible for the schizophrenic.

Noll's discussion seems to establish the shamanic journey as a unique experience that is clearly not to be confused with the schizophrenic state of consciousness. What about the initial crisis? I believe that, as is the case with the shamanic journey, the initial crisis which some shamans experience can also be differentiated from a schizophrenic state. Firstly, not all shamans experience a shamanic crisis in the form of a psychological disturbance, and secondly only a few experience a full-blown psychotic episode. However, even in the cases where psychosis does appear to exist, a diagnosis of schizophrenia seems highly unlikely. That is because the shaman's psychotic episode is short-lived and is followed by full 'recovery' of their health and psychological faculties. The majority of schizophrenics, on the other hand, do not appear to recover totally and frequently need continuous psychological support throughout their lives.

How can we then explain the prevalence of the 'schizophrenia theory'? I believe that this demonstrates the risk of allowing our judgments and cultural norms to influence our assessment and understanding of other cultures. Cultural biases can affect the way anthropologist's judge and sometime devalue the cultures that they visit. Terms such as 'primitive', 'barbaric' and 'savages' are common within the anthropological literature.

This seems particularly true in relation to states of consciousness. In the eyes of traditional western psychology any behaviour which does not fit the definition of 'norm' is usually classified as negatively deviant. Noll[22] points out that 'states of consciousness that are altered in some fashion are traditionally viewed as pathological merely because they deviate from . . . the "ordinary state" against which all other states are contrasted.' Clearly, this would explain how the initiation crisis and the shamanic journey could be perceived as abnormal and even psychotic by western researchers. However, today, even within the psychological consensus, new theories of personality proposed by scholars such as Ken Wilber[23] and James Hillman[24] among others, all suggest that 'normal' is by no means the most evolved possibility.

There are a few additional points that need to be considered when discussing shamanism and schizophrenia. One is the fact that most researchers have never had any experience of the shamanic state of consciousness. Therefore, it would be extremely difficult for them to fully understand the true nature of this state of consciousness, and as a result the true nature of shamanism.[25] In fact, some western scholars who have experienced this state, having undergone shamanic training, report acquiring a more profound understanding of shamanism and shamanic practices as a result.

Another limitation that needs to be taken into account revolves around the issue of language. Many anthropologists, both in the past and even in recent years, have relied mostly on informants and translators in their attempt to understand and study the societies they visit. So, especially when it concerns such foreign behaviours and worldviews, it is easy to see how language could have played a major role in the misunderstanding and misinterpretation of shamans and their behaviour. In 2001 I attended a small gathering led by a Palestinian dervish. Since he did not speak English, his words of wisdom were translated for me from Hebrew (which he used in honour of his Jewish–Israeli guests). At the end of a fascinating evening, as we were leaving in the early hours of the morning, this wise man approached me and apologized that he could not speak my language. He used a very creative metaphor, that has stayed with me ever since. He told me that he was sorry for not speaking English and that he did not like translations. He said, 'When you transfer food from one plate to another, it gets cold along the way; it loses heat during the movement. So it is when one is translating one language to another – some of the meaning is lost on the way.'

Finally, it is important to note that not all anthropologists perceived shamans as schizophrenic or psychologically unwell and that native people themselves do differentiate between the shamanic crisis and psychological illness. Furthermore, it has been observed that shamans are not only healthy, but appear to be even healthier than most of their community members.

In fact, shamans often end up as the most highly functional members of the community and, according to Eliade,[26] 'show proof of a more than normal nervous constitution. They achieve a degree of concentration beyond the capacity of the profane. They sustain exhausting efforts; they control their ecstatic movements, and so on.' Eliade provides an example of a Kazak Kirgiz shaman, who, when in trance, 'though he flings himself in all directions with his eyes shut, nevertheless finds all the objects that he needs.' In conclusion, the literature provides ample evidence to support the fact that shamans around the world show no sign of mental disintegration, and demonstrate cognitive abilities which surpass those of most of their community members. Thus, shamans not only recover from their initiation crisis, but attain even higher than usual levels of both psychological and physical health.

THE TRANSFORMATIVE POWER OF CRISIS

If the shaman's initiation crisis is not a mere outbreak of psychological or physical illness, what *could* be its significance? It appears that the wounding of the neophyte through illness or crisis is a necessary step in their journey to become a shaman. The question therefore arises, what is the meaning of illness and crisis within the shamanic context?

At times, great difficulties and mental breakdowns can lead us to an awakening of a new self and a new life-path. Some psychological disturbances can be regarded as developmental crises rather than as mere pathologies. Developmental crises can be defined as 'periods of psychological stress and difficulty that can accompany life transitions and turning points. They may be marked by considerable psychological turmoil, sometimes even of life-threatening proportions'.[27] Many contemporary mental health clinicians and researchers are now acknowledging that psychological disorders, including psychoses, may at times result in significant personal growth and enhanced mental and spiritual health. Thus, it seems that illness and psychological crisis can, at times, become transformative agents for growth and healing.

In fact, I find that crisis is sometimes *necessary* for spiritual and personal growth. As John Perry,[28] a Jungian psychiatrist, observed: 'spirit [is] constantly striving for release from its entrapment in routine or conventional mental structures . . . During a person's developmental process, if this work of releasing spirit becomes imperative but is not undertaken voluntarily . . . then the psyche is apt to take over and overwhelm the conscious personality . . . The individuating psyche abhors stasis as nature abhors a vacuum.'

From Perry's point of view, then, when the soul or the psyche is stuck or strangled, in order to free itself it actually generates crisis. In other words, when we are off our life-path, it could be said that our soul, higher self or inner intelligence pushes us back onto it by creating psychological or physical crisis in our lives. Thus, we are forced to look into ourselves, discover ways of healing ourselves and connect with our power.

In 1978 I developed a degenerative disease of the spine. At that time I was working as a midwife in a hospital and was not happy with my job. However, I couldn't see a way out. As time passed, my spine disease progressed until eventually I literally couldn't work any more; I couldn't lift patients or do much with my hands. Searching for a cure, I went through almost every medical intervention possible.

After a long period of sick leave I came back to work, wearing a neck collar. I was still restricted and couldn't perform my work fully, but I had no other profession and didn't know what to do. At a certain point I decided to go to the Open University, but the hours of my work were not allowing me to study properly, and I eventually stopped my studies.

One day, a friend told me that she had read an advertisement in the paper about a course in applied social studies and social work, and that mature students were encouraged to apply. My disease was leading me to despair. I couldn't do my job properly, and I was afraid that I would end up living on a disability pension. I decided to go for it and apply, and was accepted to the programme.

This door opened for me out of nowhere. I wasn't even actively searching or thinking of going to university. I believe that my neck disease pushed me back to the path I was born to tread. But that was just the first step. I went to university and became a social worker, but my neck had not healed. It had been bothering me less, since I didn't need to do any strenuous physical work, but I was still very much limited by it.

A few years after graduating from university, when I arrived in New York to work in a community centre, I came across Reiki. It was Reiki that not only healed my spine disease, but also opened a whole new world for me. Chambers opened in my mind, which I never knew existed. I became more aware of complementary medicine and other complementary forms of therapy. It was Reiki that opened the door to alternative methods of healing for me, and put me on the road that ultimately led me shamanism. To this day, I am grateful for the years I had suffered from my spine disease. For with my disease came the changes that brought me to where I am today. It was my illness that ultimately paved my way to shamanism, and to a new life.

It is important to realise, however, that crisis does not *necessarily* lead to growth. The outcome of the crisis depends very much on how it is viewed and dealt with. I believe there are two basic ways in which a crisis can be handled, depending on the way in which it is interpreted. If we perceive illness or crisis to be wrong or simply an unwanted disruption of what life *should* be, then we are likely to try to suppress it or get rid of it. In this way the growth process can be hindered or delayed. If, on the other hand, we perceive crisis and illness to be the beginning of a transformative process in our lives, then we handle it differently.

In shamanic societies, the initiation crisis is perceived to be a doorway to a new selected vocation and a valuable developmental process. The neophyte is nurtured and supported by their community members, as well as trained by the practising shaman. The shaman guides the student to make the necessary journeys, learn how to contact the spirits, and receive the appropriate healing for their role. The novice comes to understand and perceive their crisis as being healthy and positive. This helps them not only to recover their own health, but also to become a healthy and strong healer for their community. As Joan Halifax[29] eloquently summarises, 'Illness thus becomes the vehicle to a higher plane of consciousness.'

We find a beautiful example of this process in the story of Savone, an Enet woman who went berry-picking in the forest when a girl. She was found there days later, wandering about demented with a tale of how she had been attacked by a forest god. As she proved to be pregnant, and produced a stillborn child, it may be presumed that she had been raped by a stranger. Her trauma-induced madness persisted, until her family handed her over to a Ket shaman who persuaded her that she had been chosen by the spirits to become a shaman, and that the god's attack on her had been the first sign of this. With that realisation she began to recover her wits, and under the old man's training gradually turned into one of the most famous shamans of her people in the early twentieth century.[30] This can show how giving meaning to a traumatic experience is potentially healing, and more than that; the experience of the trauma is transformed into power.

SHAMAN AS THE WOUNDED HEALER

Shamans are very frequently people who have suffered much throughout their lives. This suffering may have been sudden and traumatic experiences such as that of Savone, or suffering which is intentionally sought after in the long initiatory process into shamanhood. In some cases, it is through working shamanically with others that the shaman heals and recovers from their trauma. In others, it is only after first curing themselves that the shaman is able to cure others. Having suffered themselves, shamans are the world's original 'wounded healers'.

The psychologist Carl G. Jung once said, 'Only the wounded physician heals.' According to him, in order for a healer, therapist or physician to be effective in their work, they must first experience some sort of wounding in their own lives. Clinical observations also point to the fact that people who have suffered themselves may be the best equipped, at times, to aid others relieve their own suffering. The concept of the wounded healer, however, is found not only in the writings of psychologists, but also in the myths and practices of many of the world's cultures, whether shamanic or non-shamanic.

Shamans say that in order to be able to heal a sickness, one must first *know* the sickness. On his initiatory journey, Sereptie, a Siberian Samoyed shaman, was led by his guardian spirit to meet the spirits of a certain powerful disease. In order to become a powerful shaman, Sereptie was told, he 'must be shown all the ways of diseases'.[31] The initiatory journey of yet another Samoyed shaman also contains a similar notion, as he meets in his journey 'the Lord of Madness and Lords of all the nervous disorders' as well as the spirits of smallpox and syphilis.[32]

Looking at this shamanic notion from a different perspective, it could be said that in order for a healer of any kind to be effective, they must be familiar with or be able to empathise with the state their clients are in. Thus, a healer who has never experienced pain may have difficulty understanding that of their clients. It is reasonable to assume that without having experienced any emotional turmoil throughout their lives, a healer's ability to empathise with their client and their ability to contain their experience of pain may be hindered. The wounded healer is an essential aspect of the shaman, for it is through the healed wound that they gain their ability to diagnose, to empathise and eventually to heal.

Cases of personal crisis leading to a professional path within the various healing and therapeutic arts are plentiful, and not only among shamanic cultures, but also among modern health care professionals. Often, people who have recovered from addictions go on to work therapeutically with others who are struggling with alcoholism or drug abuse. Parents who have children with physical or learning disabilities are often involved in groups and movements that are helping other families in similar circumstances. Other health care professionals report having experienced severe crisis in the form of illness, and many others have experienced wounding in the form of psychological pain and crisis.

Jeanne Achterberg[33] tells of a woman suffering from cancer, who eloquently summarised the concept of the wounded healer. In her words, 'It isn't what therapists do that is of so much importance, but rather who they are.'

Both in the case of shamans and in that of contemporary healers and therapists, it is their own healed wounds which help them to have empathy and understanding of the people that come to them for help. I can certainly see how it is true in my case, and how my own personal wounding helped me to become a better therapist and healer. My own private pain, and the process which I went through to heal it, not only enriched my own life, but also enabled me to have a more compassionate understanding of others. Connecting with my own creative power helped me to be able to not only recognise the disempowerment in others, but also to be able to help them connect with the creative power within them.

However, it is important to realise that it is not the suffering itself which makes the healer, but the healing from it. It is there that the difference between identifying with the sufferer and empathising with them lies. If a person has been wounded but did not manage to heal, they would be less likely to be able to help others heal themselves. If the healer experienced the same difficulty as the ill person but has not healed, identification will take place and the healer, rather than aiding the person, will be dragged along with them, and attempt to dismiss or avoid their experiences. However, if they experienced the pain and healed it, then empathy is more likely to be the response. The healer would then be more able to guide the person to come in touch with their own power.

It is also my own process of self-healing that has made me realise that my role is not to heal or fix people, but rather to facilitate the process of self-healing in them. It was Socrates (whose own mother had been a midwife) who likened the role of the teacher and therapist to that of the midwife. He referred to himself, in fact, as an 'intellectual midwife'. As an ex-midwife, I find that metaphor to be extremely accurate in relation to the role of the healer or shaman as well. Just as the midwife only facilitates the delivery of the baby, but does not give birth to it herself, so I believe that the healer or shaman's true role is not to cure people, but rather to assist them in their encounter with their own spirits and their own power.

APPRENTICESHIP

After answering the initial call of the spirits, the shaman-to-be now faces a long period of training. The characteristics of the training process which most shamans undergo bear certain similarities across cultures, yet we must have in mind that distinct differences also exist. For example, while some tribes would have the older shaman training the novice, in others the expectation is for the spirits to educate the neophyte directly.

During training, the neophyte receives teachings from both the ordinary reality teacher (the practising tribal shaman) and the non-ordinary reality teachers (the spirits). Very much like any medical student in the West, the teachings the neophyte receives from their shaman-teacher are composed of both theoretical and practical information. In the shamanic context these teachings consist of the cosmology of the spirit world, the cultural stories and myths, different rituals, and shamanic healing techniques. Through these teachings the neophyte learns how to interpret the images and messages they receive while journeying to the spirit world, in the context of their own cultural and shamanic traditions.

Alongside the theoretical and practical studies given by the shaman in ordinary reality, the neophyte also receives teachings and healings directly from their spirit teachers, by way of vision quest, dreaming and journeying to the spirit world. The teachings they receive by both shaman and spirits help the neophyte to connect with their inner powers and abilities and shape them into an effective shaman. By the end of this training period the neophyte is ready to serve their community as the healer and mediator between the spirit world and ordinary reality.

The apprenticeship period varies considerably from culture to culture. It can last for days, weeks, months or even as long as 20 to 30 years. In addition to learning various diagnostic and healing techniques, cultural stories and myths, and becoming competent in entering altered states of consciousness and journeying, the shaman must also meet their own helping spirits and establish a healthy and strong relationship with them, as well as acquire a good knowledge of their multi-layered world. The student needs to learn how to reach these different worlds as well as how to protect themselves while travelling there, in their search for knowledge and healing.

This is by no means an easy task. Since the student does not yet have the trained eye to see spirits, a great deal of the training involves learning how to connect with the spirit teachers, how to recognise them and to commune with them. Depending on the culture, different techniques are used to attain this initial 'spirit vision'.

The Conibo shaman, for example, in order to initiate contact with the spirits, drinks a decoction of tobacco and smokes as much as he can in a hermetically-sealed hut.[34] Antoin Biet, writing in the 1600s, provides us with an example of a South American shaman, in his first attempt to attain spirit vision:

. . . they make him dance until he is so exhausted because of the weakness caused by his fasting that he falls fainting and swooning to the ground. To revive him they put on him girdles and collars of those great black ants whose bites cause so much pain. They open his mouth by force and put in it a sort of funnel into which they pour a great Bessel full of juice drawn from tobacco. This strange medicine causes him to have vertigo and vomit blood. Its effects last several days. After such violent remedies, and such rigorous fasts, he is made a piayé and has the power of curing illnesses and evoking the Devil.[35]

Another rather drastic example of this was documented among the Enet tribe of north-west Siberia, where a neophyte shaman was simply blindfolded by two older shamans and was then beaten about the head until he was stunned into seeing spirits.[36]

Having completed their training period, the new shaman must now overcome a third and final obstacle on their way to becoming a full-fledged shaman. That is, of course, the acceptance of the shaman into the community. This final stage is perhaps the most difficult of all. The shaman may be fully accepted by the spirits and may have learned all the chants, ceremonies and oral tradition required, but could still be rejected by their people if they do not 'connect' with the shaman. This process can last for several years, as is the case with the Tapirapé Indians:

The mere fact that a young shaman had several dangerous dreams did not make him a shaman of proven ability and power. To prove himself, he had to take part in the 'fight against the beings of Thunder', and by the side of his mentor he had to perform cures. If successful, he would be called now and then by people for cures. With a reputation of several cures, and with continuous dreaming during which he had supernatural encounters, he built his reputation as a shaman over a period of many years.[37]

* * *

If some of my childhood experiences had been deathlike, then a powerful experience I had as an adult took me that one step further. I was already living in England at that time and working as a social worker when I had gone through an extremely traumatic and painful experience, which affected my life very drastically. During this painful period in my life, I was having frequent anxiety attacks, coupled with hyperventilation.

One day, while spending time with two of my friends, I had an attack, which affected my breathing severely. They were extremely alarmed and called for an ambulance. I was taken to the hospital, and my friends were driving in the car behind us. I remember lying in the ambulance and the next thing I was having a dream.

I dreamed of flying over a very high mountain, hovering over it. Over the mountain was the most beautiful scenery I had ever seen. Blue water, green pastures and trees. I was hovering over the mountain, and looking over, I could see people sitting by the river. They were looking at me, gesturing me with their hands, to go back. I decided not to join them, turned, and started to fly back.

Next, I felt a thumping on my chest and I was back in the ambulance. My friends had seen the ambulance lights flash and the sirens going off. When we reached the hospital the doctor told me, 'We lost you for a short time. Welcome back.' I asked him what he meant, and he told me, 'They radioed us, they thought you had died.' I think that that day I had died and come back, and that experience changed my life and my view about death. When I realised my experience was not a dream, I somehow lost that intense fear of dying I had been unknowingly carrying with me all that time.

3 Gateway to the Spirits: Shamanic Worlds, Shamanic Journeys

The world is as you dream it.
Numi Shaman

The shamanic journey lies at the heart of all shamanic practices around the world. The role of the shaman is to heal, help and support the people of their community. A shaman's work varies considerably – from helping a hunt to be successful, to curing depression, epilepsy or even cancer. The shaman is also in charge of retrieving lost souls, guiding the souls of the dead to their resting place and bringing power back from the spirit world. It is in this search for help and advice that the shaman embarks on their flight into the spirit world – the shamanic journey.

The experiences of the shaman may vary considerably, depending on the nature of their mission and the specific spirit helpers encountered in the different shamanic worlds. During these dream-like journeys the shaman's experiences range from the dramatic and harsh to the heavenly and ecstatic and may evoke emotions such as terror, bliss, intense love or sadness, excitement and joy, fear, peace and total trust.

The shamanic journey can be divided into three stages: first, the preparation and purification stage prior to the journey. At this stage the shaman begins to change their state of consciousness through a variety of rituals and actions. These may include periods of isolation from the community, specific fasting rituals and the practice of celibacy. The second stage is the full induction of an altered state of consciousness (ASC) and the actual shamanic journey. The third and final stage is the return of the shaman to ordinary reality, where they pass on the knowledge or power acquired on the journey to the spirit realms.

The shamanic journey is a rich and complex phenomenon and in this chapter we will explore in full detail its multiple and fascinating facets. This exploration will touch upon the process of the shamanic journey in traditional shamanic societies, as well as on the journeying process and experiences of practitioners of core shamanic counselling today. Before we can talk about the shaman's journey and its processes, however, we must first explore and understand the nature of the spirit worlds to which we journey.

TRAVERSING THE SHAMANIC LANDSCAPE

Shamans journey to the worlds of the spirits in their quest for knowledge, power and healing. In the first chapter I briefly discussed the cosmology of the spirit world. In this chapter we take further steps into the realm of the spirits, to explore and get to know it on a deeper level. As previously mentioned, the shaman's universe is comprised of three basic layers, or worlds – the upper, middle and lower worlds. Some cultures consider the upper and lower worlds themselves to be multi-layered.

Among some of the Siberian tribes, the supreme ruler Bai Ulgen was thought to live on the uppermost levels of the upper world. The lower world, on the other hand, was often considered to be inhabited by the souls of the dead. Both upper and lower worlds are at the same time similar yet different to our familiar ordinary reality. While, for example, the lower world might be comprised of landscapes which are identical to those of our world, it is possible for the time of day to be different between these two worlds. While it is night in our reality, it is possible for the sun to be shining in the lower world. The normal physical laws of ordinary reality do not apply in the shamanic world. People may find that they can fly, travel vast distances, walk on water or swim under water without the need for any equipment. There could be two suns in the sky, mountains may walk and the sea could be red. And since everything is alive and with spirit, when journeying one can speak and interact with virtually anything – a tree, a river, a bird, an animal and even stones.

These three worlds are generally believed to be interconnected by a central world axis, or *axis mundi*. This axis passes through a hole or an opening through which the soul of the shaman is able to travel to the upper and lower worlds. This symbolic connection between the different worlds takes, according to Eliade,[1] three main forms. The first is the 'world pillar' – an image which likens the universe to a tent or house, in which the sky is supported by a central pillar. The second is the 'cosmic mountain', representing the centre of the world. The third is the 'world tree', located at the centre of the earth, and symbolising life, creation, fertility, regeneration and immortality. It is interesting to note that these symbols are found in the myths of many different cultures around the world, both shamanic and non-shamanic. One such striking example is the tree of life which is a symbol found in the Jewish Kabbala.

Some may regard the spirit world to be a mere mental construction, or to reside within our own subconscious mind. Shamans, however, consider the spirit world to be just as real as our ordinary waking reality. For the shaman, this world exists independently of our mind, although the mind is the means through which it is accessed. Prem Das, a Huichol shaman, provides one such view on shamanic travel: 'There is a doorway within our minds that usually remains hidden and secret until the time of death. The Huichol word for it is *nieríka. Nieríka* is a cosmic portway or interface between so-called ordinary and non-ordinary realities. It is a passageway and at the same time a barrier between worlds.'[2] The spirit world, then, is not a place located in a different space, but rather a world located in a *different state of consciousness*, existing parallel to our ordinary reality. One of the main skills that shamans learn in their practice is how to be able to change their state of consciousness at will, to become aware of this alternative reality.

GAINING ACCESS TO THE SPIRIT WORLDS

Up until now we have explored the different realms we can visit in shamanic journeys. The main tool the shaman uses to enter those invisible realms is the alteration of their state of consciousness. Throughout the centuries, shamans in different cultures have developed and used different techniques to induce an altered state of consciousness (ASC). It is important to note, however, that shamans are not alone in their quest to gain access to these states. Mystics and spiritual aspirants throughout the world have also sought to attain ASC in their practice. Mystical traditions explain and teach that it is while being in this state that one gains profound realisations and wisdom.

The shamanic state of consciousness (SSC), however, has unique characteristics of its own that differentiates it from other altered states of consciousness to be found in different spiritual and mystical practices. Furthermore, although it is similar to other states of consciousness such as dreaming and hypnosis, it is still significantly different from these states as well. After analysing the shamanic practices in 42 cultures, Peters and Price-Williams[3] concluded that the SSC is a unique type of ASC and that it is different from other similar states such as dreaming, meditation, hypnosis or drug-induced hallucinatory states. Roger Walsh[4] provides a thorough discussion on this subject.

However, to whatever degree the SSC is similar or dissimilar to other such states, one thing is clear – while in SSC the shaman has access to resources that are otherwise inaccessible in our normal waking state of consciousness. I believe that while in a normal state of consciousness we are trapped in our logical mind. Hence, when we try to gain understanding or healing for ourselves and others, our resources are limited by it. The shaman, when entering an ASC, is leaving the boundaries of the mind and relying on other resources to gain healing and knowledge – resources that are external to their mind.

The shaman would call these resources 'spirits'. Others may call them our subconscious mind. However, it is not the terminology which is important in this case. Whether we believe that our soul is entering the spirit worlds or that we are journeying into the archives of our unconscious mind is not the real issue. It is rather the fact that these resources are unknown and are external to our waking critical mind. Shamans are able to pass through the crack in the wall of our conscious mind, past the barriers between self and non-self, and enter into the realm of the spirit which lies beyond our intellect. It is this passage that is facilitated through the alteration of our state of consciousness.

We have established that in order for shamans to journey and carry out their healing work, they must first alter the state of their normal waking consciousness. In order to help us understand the way shamanic states are induced, let us review a theory proposed by Charles Tart.[5] This theory is aimed at explaining the different stages characterising the induction of altered states of consciousness.

The three stages described by Tart are: destabilisation of the initial state of consciousness, followed by a second, transitory stage of re-patterning, and a final stabilisation stage of the new state.

During the first stage, the regular patterns of our mind and brain are disrupted by different destabilising forces – these are the specific techniques used by the shaman to induce the altered state which may include certain types of music and drumming, sleep deprivation, acute hunger or the ingestion of psychedelics.

When reaching sufficient intensity, these destabilising forces disrupt the usual state of consciousness and the transition to the altered state of consciousness is set in motion. The quality or characteristics of this altered state depend very much on the effects of several factors on the brain and mind. Some of these factors are: the tools being used to induce the ASC, the intention and belief system of the person, and their physiological state. When this transition towards the new altered state is finished, the third stage of the process is brought on, as consciousness restabilises itself into the new and altered state of consciousness.

The ability to enter altered states of consciousness is a skill which can be acquired and one which improves with practice. This means that the more practiced and experienced a shaman is at entering altered states, the more easily and rapidly they are able to reach that state. With time, the shaman's need for techniques to facilitate the transition to an ASC may lessen. Not only that, but the more experienced the shaman becomes, the more 'accessible' the spirit world may be for them, even in ordinary waking reality. This means that visions and messages which could formerly be acquired only while in an altered state of consciousness may become partially accessible to the shaman even in waking reality.

A few years ago I actually had the privilege of experiencing a journey unaided by the sound of the drums. During one of my stays in Israel, I decided to go on a morning walk in the woods close to the place where I was staying. Although this was not the first time I had been in these woods, for some reason I got lost and could not find my way out. It seemed like any direction I took only brought me further and further in. On my way I saw many caves, which indicated to me that I was definitely not on my path back home. I was lost. After an hour of wandering, attempting to find my way back, I decided to try and connect with my guardian spirit and ask for help. I closed my eyes and started breathing, attempting to take myself into an altered state of consciousness. I visualised myself in my power place and called my guardian spirit. As always, he was there. He laughed and asked me to follow him. I opened my eyes, stood up, and he was in front of me, guiding my steps. Before long, I was back on a familiar path, heading home.

In Chapter 1 I briefly mentioned the varied means by which shamans attain an altered state of consciousness and journey to the spirit worlds. Now, let us take a closer look at the variety of means by which shamans have traditionally brought on an alteration in their state of consciousness.

INDUCING ALTERED STATES OF CONSCIOUSNESS

The techniques and rituals used by shamans to reach the desired altered state are extremely varied, and are generally geared towards either over-stimulation or deprivation of different sensory systems. These techniques make use of both physiological and psychological mechanisms in order to create an ASC. Some of the more psychological techniques are commonly used prior to the actual journey, and include periods of solitude, contemplation and prayer, as well as the creation of the appropriate mindset and environmental setting that are conducive for the success of the journey. Following are some examples of the more common techniques used in different shamanic societies for the purpose of entering an altered state of consciousness and visiting the world of the spirits.

Physical and sensory deprivation

A common group of techniques used by shamans throughout the world is based on the principal of either physical or sensory deprivation. One of these techniques is fasting, which may sometimes extend to the degree of even avoiding drinking water. The number of days of the fast varies from culture to culture and may also be determined by the seriousness of the client's condition. At times, fasting prior to shamanic work is required not only from the shaman but also from the person seeking the help.

Another technique used is sleep deprivation, where the shaman avoids sleeping for several nights prior to journeying. Abstinence from sex is also used among many shamanic cultures as a means of altering states of consciousness and preserving energy. By conserving sexual energy, the novice shaman acquires additional power, which can then be redirected towards healing and learning. This practice also exists among many non-shamanic traditions, such as Hinduism and Buddhism. Novice shamans throughout the world are at times required to abstain from sex for long periods in order for them to become effective shamans.

The shaman may also alter their state of consciousness by using techniques of sensory deprivation. Journeying and other ceremonies are conducted under conditions of darkness. This means conducting the journey either during times of twilight or night, or by artificially creating darkness, by darkening the environment and covering the eyes. It could be said that by curtaining off the outside world, the inner senses become more acute and the shaman can see and hear the spirits more clearly. Other forms of sensory deprivation include restriction of movement and gazing for long periods of time into the flames of a fire.

Temperature conditions

Exposure to extreme temperature conditions is also used by some shamanic cultures as a means of inducing ASC. Two popular techniques are exposure to extreme cold or extreme heat. One technique which involves exposure to extreme heat and has gained popularity amongst westerners is that of the sweat lodge.* The traditional use of the sweat lodge is found mainly among the North American Indian tribes. There are specific rituals that are conducted prior to entering the sweat lodge and during the time spent in it. While in the lodge the shaman may recite specific chants and burn certain herbs while listening to the beat of the drum. The use of the sweat lodge can be physically taxing, and include effects such as nausea, rapid pulse rate, dizziness or even fainting.

Hallucinogenic plants

Hallucinogenic plants are another common tool used by shamans to enter ASC. Many people tend to associate shamanism with the use of hallucinogenic drugs. However, hallucinogens are by no means the most dominant tool used by shamans to enter altered states. The use of hallucinogens is to be found mainly in South America and certain parts of Siberia. The range of hallucinogenic plants used by shamans throughout the world is impressive. Some 100 different types of drugs have been identified so far and the shamanic use of such plants is thought to have existed for more than 3,000 years.

Particularly common in South and Central America is the use of *yage* (also known as *ayahuasca*) – a drink brewed from the banisteriopsis vine. Both the shaman and the person seeking help, as well the tribe's people attending the shamanic ceremony, partake in the drinking of the brew. The use of the peyote cactus (referred to by Don Juan as *mescalito*, and containing the active ingredient mescaline) is also to be found in the Americas. The Huichol embark upon a

---

* A typical sweat lodge is a small structure, made of wood and covered with heavy waterproof material to prevent heat from escaping. Red hot stones are placed in a pit in the centre of the lodge and cold water is periodically poured on the stones, in order to produce steam. Usually certain herbs are also burnt inside the lodge, for their sacred significance and for purification.

journey to the sacred lands of the peyote, where the plant is ceremoniously harvested from the desert soil. A number of cactus buttons are then chewed by the shaman or the journeyer until the desired effect is brought on. Forms of the powerful and dangerous plant datura and different kinds of hallucinogenic mushrooms are used both in the Americas and Europe.

The most common mushroom used by Siberians is the *amanita muscaria* or agaric. The *psilocybe* mushroom, also called 'the flesh of the gods', is used widely in Mexico. The Mazatec shaman Maria Sabina is famous for her mushroom-induced journeys in which she speaks with the voice of the mushrooms themselves. When asked from where her messages came, she would reply: it was not me who said it, but the mushroom. Although we would consider the active ingredients found in these hallucinogenic plants to be the ones responsible for generating the shaman's experiences while on a journey, shamans themselves believe that it is rather the sacred spirit of the plant which is aiding them while in an ASC. It is the spirit of the plant that talks to them in the form of the visions that they see.[6]

By using the sacred plants the shaman is able to experience the expansion of the boundaries of the self, an enhanced awareness of the unity of life and a sense of awe and wonder, enabling them to access the realms beyond the confines of their mind and senses. However, unlike the mystics of other spiritual practices, shamans do not seek enlightenment for its sake alone, but rather as a means of healing and helping their community. Thus, hallucinogenic plants are revered and honoured as the vehicles in their quest for healing.

Hallucinogenic plants are considered to be sacred in shamanic societies, as they are the portal that enables the shaman to access the world of the spirits. Shamans understand the power of the plants, they know the spirit of the plants and they respect it. Thus, the shamanic use of these plants is restricted only for the purpose of entering and journeying. No shaman would ever use a hallucinogenic plant for recreational purposes as westerners do. Furthermore, shamans know how much of the drug to take, and in what form, in order for them to remember the content of the journey and the messages received from the spirits, and still retain some awareness of their surroundings.

Auditory stimulation

The spirit world is closely tied to music. Monotonous rhythmic stimulation is one of the most common and ancient means used by shamans all over the world to enter into an altered state of consciousness. Drumming, rattling, dancing, chanting, singing and monotonous body movements are some of the main techniques used. One of the most common tools is the 'power song'. These songs are given to the shaman by their own spirit helpers, either during an initial period of solitude, while on a journey or while dreaming. In some cultures the song would not be exclusive to the shaman but would be a shared chant or song of the tribe. Just like the drumbeat, power songs tend to be repetitive and monotonous, thus assisting the shaman to enter an ASC.

Dancing is also a technique that has long been used in many cultures, both shamanic and non-shamanic, to enter altered states. Examples include the dancing dervishes and the Siberian shamans. Among some of the shamans of Siberia, dancing prior to journeying also facilitates a transition to an ASC, due to the fact that an assortment of bells and other metallic objects sewn to the shaman's outfit jingle while they dance, thus creating an auditory beat to accompany the beat created by the movements of the dancing body. The most important tools used for entering ASC, however, and perhaps the most central and universal to shamanic practices, are the shaman's drum and rattle.

The shaman's drum

The drum and the rattle are the shaman's companions, *par excellence*, facilitating their transportation into the non-ordinary realms of reality. It appears that a drum beating at a rhythm of approximately 200 to 220 beats per minute is especially effective in inducing an altered state of consciousness. The steady and monotonous beat of the drum not only helps the shaman to enter SSC, but also helps them to maintain this state of consciousness throughout the journey. In order to enter SSC, the shaman would either start drumming and then allow their assistant to take over the drumming while the shaman is journeying (as among many Siberian tribes), or alternatively, the assistant would be doing the drumming from beginning to end.

The symbolic meaning of the shaman's drum reaches far beyond the mere sound it produces. The North Siberians, for example, use the skin of a reindeer to make their drums and it is on the back of that reindeer that the shaman symbolically rides on their journey to the spirit worlds.

Several mechanisms could be referred to when trying to explain the effects of the drum on human consciousness. First, the sound of the drum could be functioning as a kind of sensory blocking device, focusing the journeyer on the journey and their mission, directing their attention away from any external stimulations that might disturb their journey. It is speculated that the monotonous sound of the drum may actually create a kind of 'blocking' effect on a neurological brain level, which causes any other sensory stimuli, including pain, to be filtered out of our consciousness. In this state the shaman's mind is free to explore the world of the spirits. This might be further supported by what I witness in my work with people. Clients who find it difficult to let go and journey and who are very much in their mind, find it difficult to go totally into an ASC. These people often say to me, 'Make the sound of the drum very high, so that my thoughts don't disturb me.'

Another explanation of how drumming may induce an ASC is proposed by Tart.[7] He claims that drumming and loud noises may change our usual state of consciousness simply by disrupting the on-going psychological processes that maintain this usual state. A strong enough drum beat can act as a destabilising agent, and create an alteration in the state of consciousness very quickly and easily. This process could be likened to being 'startled' into an altered state.

Finally, it is commonly believed that the sound of drumming alters brainwave patterns. Neher[8] proposed that drumming at a certain frequency could enhance theta rhythms in certain areas of the brain. These very same brainwaves are also the ones related to creativity, vivid imagery and unusual problem-solving.

THE POWER PLACE

In order for the shaman to journey to the spirits, they also need to have a specific place to journey *from* – a place from where they can either dive into the earth or soar into the sky. In core shamanic practices we refer to this place as 'the power place'.

The power place is a doorway leading or connecting the ordinary reality to the non-ordinary reality. It could be a place one has experienced in childhood, adolescence, or even adulthood. It is important that this place is not imaginary, or a place we read about, or saw in a film. It has to be a real place in ordinary reality, which we have experienced for ourselves. Commonly, the power place is located in nature, is a place where one feels at home, and one which when we think about, fills us with feelings of power, joy and confidence. It should also preferably be a place where one can gain easy access to both the lower or upper worlds. Some of the power places chosen by different people I have worked with throughout the years are a tree, the sea, a mountain, a cave, and at times even man-made openings, such as mine shafts or wells.

It is important for the power place to exist in ordinary reality for two reasons. One is that it holds a true experience of power for us, and the second is that by travelling to the spirit world from a place which exists in ordinary reality, we are making that transition more clear for our psyche, and fully experience the passage of leaving one type of reality and entering another.

LOWER WORLD JOURNEYS

Most westerners are already somewhat familiar with the concept of the lower world journey, through the popular story of *Alice in Wonderland*, where Alice enters another world by going down a rabbit hole. To travel to the lower world the shaman or journeyer would usually visualise an opening in the ground, located in their power place, into which they would dive.

The nature of the actual opening differs from culture to culture, and even from person to person. For example, the entrance to the lower world among the California Indian shamans is frequently a hot spring, or alternately a hollow tree stump. The hollow tree is also popularly used by the Arunta of Australia, while the Conibo Indians follow the roots of a tree in their journey to the lower world. Other entrances include rabbit, fox or snake holes in the ground, caves, water holes, wells, or any other holes or cracks in the earth to be found in nature. In certain North American tribes shamans even create a man-made hole to facilitate their descent to the lower world.

Sereptie, a Samoyed shaman of Siberia, tells of his first experience of descending into the lower world during his initiatory experience. After felling a tree, a figure of a man jumped out of its roots, inviting Sereptie to follow him into the earth: 'As I looked round, I noticed a hole in the earth. My companion asked: "What hole is this? If your destiny is to make a drum of this tree, find it out!"; I replied: "It is through this hole that the shaman receives the spirit of his voice." The hole became larger and larger. We descended through it and arrived at a river with two streams flowing in opposite directions.'[9]

After seeing themselves entering the hole in the ground, the journeyer usually finds themselves in some kind of tunnel or a tube, leading them into the depths of the earth. Although the tunnel is dark, the journeyer is able to see the way. From my experience, and the experience of the many people I have worked with, the journey down the tunnel differs each time. Sometimes the tunnel leads directly into the landscape of the lower world. At other times, one might encounter an opening to the right or left which leads into another tunnel that eventually opens into a landscape. The landscapes encountered in the lower world are extremely varied, and resemble the landscapes found in our ordinary reality. One can emerge into a forest, at the bottom of the sea, in a desert, in a jungle with waterfalls, mountains, rivers or lakes. In this world one interacts with the spirits of nature – animals, plants, humans and even the elements, the stars, the moon and the sun.

Just as the different shamanic worlds have different landscapes and are inhabited by different kinds of teachers and spirits, so does their function differ. The shaman travels to either one of the worlds depending on their intention and mission. Although in the lower world the shaman may encounter challenges and be put to the test by the spirits (as we demonstrated in the previous chapter), it is also the place where healing and power are to be found. The lower world is where the shaman encounters power animals and possibly receives instructions for healing. It is also the place where lost souls are frequently found and brought back from. The shaman, and anyone who undertakes a shamanic journey, will journey to the lower world to obtain power and healing, whether for themselves or for others.

I feel that there is one point regarding the lower world which needs to be addressed. Throughout the years of my shamanic work I have come to realise that many people, when first learning of the concept of the lower world, associate it with the underworld or hell. Consequently, these people often fear to go on a journey to the lower world. One woman with whom I worked was extremely reluctant to journey to the lower world, in spite of my explanations and reassurance that it is safe to do so. It took her several attempts until she actually managed to descend under the ground. A man I once worked with could see the tunnel beneath his feet but was desperately hanging to the roots of the tree in his power place, trying to avoid falling into the lower world. He later explained to me that he was afraid he would come out in the land of the dead. It is very important to understand that the lower world, despite any infernal connotations which it may have for westerners, is not a dangerous or even scary place, at all. All the people I have ever worked with always found the lower world (once they reached it) to be a beautiful and safe place.

Healing journeys

A lower world journey may be undertaken with the purpose of receiving healing for a specific problem in our lives. This may be a spiritual, psychological or physical ailment we may be suffering from. Although in certain cases a healing journey alone may not be sufficient, and may need to be accompanied by other forms of shamanic work, at times a single journey may on its own bring about the necessary change.

Although I used to be a social smoker, I would also use cigarettes as a crutch. Whenever I was experiencing a difficult time in my life I would start to literally chain smoke. Once the problem was resolved I would return to my normal social smoking habits. One day I decided that I did not want to have this crutch in my life any more. I decided to go on a journey and ask for a healing for the cause of using smoking as a crutch. I present the essence of my journey here.

My guardian spirit and I journeyed to the lower world and followed our usual path to the beach which is my usual healing place. The old lady, my healer, was waiting for me, sitting in front of the fire. My second healer, who is a young man, was also present, standing next to the fire. Since I was relatively new to shamanism, I was questioning whether I was imagining this healing place, since whenever I went for healings in the past I always found myself on that same beach. I asked my healer what was the reason for that. She looked at me with sad eyes and said, 'How many hospitals do you have in your city, my child?' I felt very humbled and with tears in my eyes I asked her to forgive me for not trusting. The healing I received on this journey was quite a harsh one. My healer sat behind me while I was facing the fire and with a very sharp knife cut my back right in the middle, down the spine. She peeled off my skin and flesh very carefully, until my lungs were exposed. I could see my lungs covered with lumps of what looked like black blood clots, which she began to clean. When she finished cleaning the blood clots she began cleaning the pus which was revealed underneath. My other healer then held his hands over the lungs and colourful energy radiated from his hands, entering my lungs. In my physical body I felt trembling and tingling sensations all over. The old woman then closed me up again. I was put in a cocoon of white light and both my healers kept breathing into me, through the top of my head. I kept crying, until it was time for me to come back.

Although I had been a smoker for many years prior to doing the journey, I was able to completely stop smoking immediately following it and have not used cigarettes ever since. However, at this point I wish to note that a healing in the lower world may take a variety of forms other than the one presented in my journey. While some people may experience being cut into pieces, burned or boiled, and having their body organs replaced, others may simply be shown images, given messages or go through experiences of different sorts.

One man I once worked with was shown flashes of different childhood photos and scenes as part of his healing journey. The form of the healing one receives varies considerably from person to person and is also dependent to a large degree on the presenting problem.

At times, especially when dealing with chronic or persisting problems, the shaman would go on a healing journey on behalf of the person seeking help. I had been suffering for over 20 years from recurring attacks of pneumonia and pleurisy. Six years ago I attended a shamanic course with my teacher, at the end of which he usually performed a healing ritual. At the time of the course, I had been quite ill and my teacher's spirits instructed him to perform the healing on me. This healing ritual took place at the end of the course and involved all of the course participants. Prior to the actual ceremony, each of the participants, including myself, journeyed to ask for specific instructions as to how to prepare and dress for the healing. During the healing ceremony I had to lie on the floor while the rest of the participants stood in a circle around me. My teacher then energetically closed the circle by rattling the group together and began rattling me, while the group rattled and drummed all around us. When he could not rattle any more, my teacher lay beside me and started his journey to the spirit world, asking for healing for me, while the rest of the group, standing in a circle with their eyes closed, received messages from their own spirit helpers to aid me in my healing. I present here my teacher's account of the healing journey he had performed for me.

Journeying to the lower world, he reached a desert, where he met his healers and teachers. He could see me lying on the ground and was told by his healers to sit aside and watch while a pack of wild dogs ate my flesh. The dogs ate my inner organs first and especially my lungs before continuing to eat my outer flesh. All the while my teacher was made to sit still and watch. When the dogs finished consuming my flesh, all that remained of me was a skeleton. My teacher was then allowed to come closer to me. He saw a white bird standing next to me and was allowed to put the bird in my rib cage. My body was reconstructed until I was back to normal. We then went to the beach and I started swimming. I was joined by a school of porpoises and I continued to swim with them. My teacher was told by the spirits that I must learn from the porpoises how to live. Just as the porpoises swim, rest and eat fish, he was told that from now on I would need to swim, rest and take care of myself and start eating fish.

It has been six years since that healing journey and I have never had any recurring attacks of either pneumonia, pleurisy or any other problem with my lungs since.

THE GUARDIAN SPIRIT

In core shamanic practices, the first journey undertaken is to the lower world, in search of one's guardian spirit. In order to venture into the unknown land of the spirits, the shaman must have a guide. This role is mostly fulfilled by a spirit in the form of an animal or some other element of nature, such as the sun, a tree or even a flower. Although most commonly the guardian spirit manifests itself in the form of an animal, some interesting cases are documented of shamans possessing guardian spirits of more abstract forms. Don Handleman[10] tells of Henry Rupert, a Washo shaman of North America, who had the spirit of water as his spirit power. In his healing work he would usually receive messages and images involving the presence or absence of water, to indicate the state of health of the person he was working with.

At times, the guardian spirit or spirit ally might even metamorphose to appear in the form of a human being. Some shamans are even known to have as their spirit guides people who actually lived on earth at one time. One such case is of the Mexican 'psychic surgeon' Doña Pachita, whose guide was the last great Aztec prince Cuahutemoc (or in her words 'brother Cuahutemoc'), who would actually possess the woman's body during her unusual and powerful healing procedures.[11]

Jonathan Horwitz, with whom I studied core shamanism refers to this particular guiding spirit as 'the guardian spirit'. Many other shamanic practitioners would refer to it instead as the 'power animal'. These two terms are actually used interchangeably among the North American tribes. When reading anthropological literature we encounter other different terminologies in reference to the guardian spirit. Anthropologists exploring the Siberian tribes referred to these spirit guides as 'tutelary spirits', while in literature about Australian tribes we encounter the term 'assistant totem'. The guardian spirit may also be referred to as a 'familiar' or 'companion'. However, in core shamanic practices the guardian spirit serves a somewhat different role than that of power animals. A full discussion concerning power animals will follow in Chapter 5.

The question of when we acquire our guardian spirit is not a straightforward one. When first journeying to meet their guardian spirit, people receive varied answers to this question. At times the guardian spirit explains that it had been accompanying the person from birth, other times it reminds the person of a traumatic or difficult experience earlier on in their life and explains it had come to their aid at that particular period. People of shamanic cultures around the world believe that whether we are aware of it or not, we all have a guardian spirit and we acquire it very early on in our lives. The Jivaro, for example, believe that children would not survive into adulthood without it. These notions may seem foreign to us at first, but the fact is that the idea of having a guardian spirit is not as foreign as it may seem. Many modern westerners believe they have guardian angels or that some divine entity or power takes care of them.

For the shaman, however, the guardian spirit is more than just a protective power. Among the Salish tribe of North America, the shaman is initiated by an animal spirit, who then becomes their guardian spirit. The initiate would have to go through many rituals of purification and isolation until the animal that would become their guardian spirit appeared to them in a dream, promising its help to the future shaman. It is said that when an animal initiates a shaman, it teaches them its language and gives them a song that is to be kept secret. Among many South American cultures it is believed that the soul of the shaman can actually transform into an animal or a bird. This allows the shaman to attain intimacy with nature, thus granting them great powers.

The Kalinia of the Orinoco area of Venezuela believe that all human souls have an animalistic aspect. They call this aspect of the soul the 'double' or 'friend'. Each person's animal soul maintains a connection with its own animal family (meaning, other animals of the same species or kind), while residing with the person. Thus, every person, in addition to their human family, also has an invisible animal family. This animal family is a powerful natural spirit which guards and protects the person.[12]

No shaman can shamanise without a guardian spirit, and likewise, no modern practitioners of core shamanism would venture on a journey without it. The guardian spirit has multiple and important roles to perform in any shamanic journey. It is familiar with the terrain of the spirit worlds and so is a reliable guide to these realms. It also accompanies and protects the shaman or journeyer on their expedition to the spirit world, assists them in finding the portholes into the spirit realms, makes sure that they are not lost, and that they return to their power place at the end of the journey. The use of the word 'protect' here could sound as if the spirit world is a dangerous place. However, the type of protection I refer to is not a protection from harm or malevolent beings that might reside in the spirit world. Rather, the protection is in the form of guidance – meaning the guardian spirit leads the journeyer to the right places for them to complete the mission of their journey.

Another protective role fulfilled by the guardian spirit is to guide the journeyer back from the spirit realms and into the ordinary reality, especially if the experience of the non-ordinary reality is so wonderful that the person is somewhat reluctant to return. At times the guardian spirit may also assume the role of a spirit teacher when appropriate or necessary. And finally, regardless of any function that a guardian spirit may fulfil, it always plays a key role in each person's process of healing. From my experience, the bonding that takes place between the individual and the guardian spirit can have tremendous healing power in its own right.

Although, as mentioned above, the guardian spirit may appear in a variety of forms, when it takes the form of an animal it is always a wild animal, rather than a domesticated one. In shamanic cultures, it is believed that domesticated animals have lost their power and therefore cannot serve as a power animal or guardian spirit. However, other than that, I do not believe that certain animals are more powerful than others. The symbolic representation of the guardian spirit is a personal one and the power of the particular guardian spirit does not depend on the animal's size or species. For example, a guardian spirit in the form of a lion is not more powerful than one in the form of a mouse. It is the spirits that decide in which animal form to reveal themselves to us. I believe that the guardian spirit takes the form of an animal whose essence and spiritual power is related or connected to the person on some deep level of their existence.

My own personal experience of my guardian spirit was an interesting one. In 1987 I was attending a course in Eriksonian hypnosis. During the course I went through a very powerful and deep process that took me back to my childhood. At the end of the process I was asked, 'If you could have an animal image to help and support you when you feel powerless, what would it be?' Although I never had any special connection with or affection for elephants, it was the image of an elephant that immediately came to my mind. Exactly ten years later, while attending my first shamanic workshop and dancing with my rattle, an elephant joined me in my dance. Later on in the workshop, when I first journeyed to find my guardian spirit, I met the elephant that had danced with me. He introduced himself and told me of an incident which happened when I was a baby and I was in danger of dying. It was then that he had first entered my life, to become my guardian spirit. I have heard many similar stories from others I have worked with through the years. It is not uncommon for guardian spirits to refer to crucial times or even life-threatening situations in our lives, when asked how long they have been with us. People are often touched or become emotional when they first learn of that first encounter from their guardian spirit.

However, at times, people express surprise or even disappointment after meeting their guardian spirit for the first time. Sometimes they are surprised that their guardian spirit did not appear in the form of their favourite animal or the animal they are most connected to. At other times, their guardian spirit comes in the form of their favourite animal and they feel disappointed, thinking that they have failed to journey and imagined the animal or made it up. At yet other times, people simply encounter a guardian spirit in the form of an animal that they do not like or are afraid of, or even judge that animal not to be good enough to be their guardian spirit.

These initial feelings of confusion or disappointment soon dissipate as the person continues journeying and forms a relationship and a bond with their guardian spirit. Developing a deep relationship with one's guardian spirit is paramount to success in shamanic work. Without the spirits there is no shaman, and the guardian spirit is the first teacher to facilitate and help the shaman traverse the spirit world.

UPPER WORLD JOURNEYS

Just as the shaman dives into the ground in order to reach the lower world, so they soar into the skies in their attempt to reach the upper world. The notion of a porthole or an opening in the sky which leads to the upper world is a common theme in the myths and stories of many shamanic societies. The Yakut believe that the stars of the night skies are holes in the 'great tent' of the sky, with the Milky Way as the central seam of this tent. Among the Warao of the Amazonian forests it is believed that the Star of Dawn is the gateway to the upper world. The openings themselves are invisible to the naked eye but the shaman or journeyer, assisted by their guardian spirit and while in an ASC, is able to see and pass through them.

The shaman may begin their journey upward by climbing a ladder or a rope, a tree, a mountain, a rainbow, or even a whirlwind, as in the case of Dorothy in *The Wizard of Oz* – a story which could be easily interpreted as an upper world journey. These are all images which could be said to symbolically represent the world axis mentioned by Eliade. At other times, the shaman may journey to the upper world by transforming into a bird and flying to the sky.

Among the native people of Australia, the shaman climbs a cord or rope, which leads them up to the sky. The Warao story of the creation of the world tells of the Bahanarotu ('the shaman of light') who, when he was only 4 years old, travelled to the house of smoke in the upper world. In order to be able to fly to the sky, the child asked his father to light a fire under his hammock (after five days of complete fasting), and then rose up to the upper realms, carried by the smoke and heat vapours emitted by the fire.[13]

Just like entering the lower world through the opening at the end of the tunnel in the ground, so in upper world journeys one finds oneself either going through some opening in the sky or passing a screen or a gateway. There is always some sort of symbolic doorway which takes the journeyer into the magical realm of the upper world, be it passing through a star, a screen of clouds, or some sort of road or tube in the sky. For example, a person I once worked with would have a ladder going up into the sky, which would gradually spiral and turn into a sort of tube out of which she would soar into the upper world. Another person I have worked with experienced his entrance to the upper world by passing through a dark hole or tunnel with a light at the end of it. The tunnel was lit by small lights and seemed endless, and when he finally reached the end he found himself surrounded in bright light and in front of his teacher.

When we journey to the upper world, we do so to receive information, wisdom and teachings from the spirits. The problem for which we seek help may be psychological, spiritual or physical. The upper world is also the place of creativity, inspiration and high ideals. This world is distinctly different from the middle and lower worlds. Here, the shaman encounters teachers in the form of religious, historical or ancestral figures. In addition to human teachers, the shaman may receive teachings from clouds, stars, the moon, the sun, and different unusual or legendary animals.

Much like the lower world, the upper world is also multilayered, and the shaman is able to travel between the different layers at will, or occasionally with the help of specific spirit helpers. For example, for me to meet a certain teacher in the upper world, who advises me on psychological issues,

I need to move from one level to a higher one in the upper world. To do this I ride on the back of Pegasus, who always comes to collect me at a certain point, to which I travel on the back of my guardian spirit.

The landscapes of the upper world are not those of natural scenery to be found in our own world, but rather, more celestial. The colours are pastel; people come across castles, palaces and gardens. The Yakut believe that the upper world has a separate sun and moon, that the houses are made of iron and that the spirits in the sky have raven heads and human bodies. Upon reaching the upper world, the Bahanarotu shaman of the Warao was met with a bridge made of smoke ropes and beds of tobacco flowers in the colours of the rainbow, dancing in the light breeze, leading him to a house made of smoke.

Upper world journeys taken by modern practitioners of core shamanism are also varied and unexpected. There is no one formula for an upper world journey. The following journey was done by a 24-year-old woman, and is a beautiful example of an upper world journey taken to ask for teachings and information:

My mission on this journey is to ask my spirit helpers in the upper world what is stopping me from expressing my truth and how I can make it better. I am in my power place. My guardian spirit, Tiki, joins me. We greet each other and start flying. I am holding his hand and we are shooting up to the sky. I see a star in front of his finger and he suddenly opens his hand and we are standing somewhere, on a black stone, which is floating on a chocolate river. I see a man wearing black. 'Hello,' I say. He shakes my hand and helps me off the black stone. I am standing on the grass in front of him. *'Who are you? Are you here to help me?'* He grabs my collar and tells me, *'Come.'* We start walking. *'I am going to show you the way.'* He tells me his name is Tom. He points to the sky and it's like fire. *'Where are you taking me?'* I ask him. *'We are going to help you find the way. I am taking you somewhere else. Be patient and follow me.'* We reach a big stone road with a gate at the end of it. Tom tells me to go to the gate. I stand by the gate and an angel appears. She is wearing a gold outfit and tells me her name is Sarah. She is holding a magic wand in her hand and we are flying together. We reach a cliff and stand on the edge of it, as if we are going to fall off. And as we are looking across I see a city, all gray and foggy. We can't see. *'Where are we?'* I ask. *'You are looking across to the future. Come with me.'* We are flying through the clouds and land on an ice glacier. It's very cold and I am sitting on the glacier, with my feet in the water. I am cold. Tiki is holding my hand as we start flying, and Sarah is directing our way, pointing ahead with her magic wand. We fly and finally we reach my teacher. We are standing somewhere, looking at the world, and we are surrounded by darkness and stars. *'I am here to seek your help . . .'* *'I know. Come and sit down.'* I sit next to him, looking at the world. *'I need your help; I want to know how I can express my truth and make my communication better.'* He points at the stars. *'You see?'* We are now sitting in a cinema, watching The Wizard of Oz. *'It all begins from your childhood and you need to see and realise everything.'* The film stops, the cinema is dark. *'You need to see and realise that everything is like the movies.'* I am confused. The film is now playing again in the background. *'You need to see.'* He points at the Wizard of Oz. *'You need to see and realise.'* He now has Toto the dog in his arms and he is petting him. *'You need to see and realise that you are the one who matters and that you are the one.*

You need to see, you need to feel, and you need to feel the love and the happiness.' We are watching Judy Garland, the part with the yellow brick road. My teacher is still petting the dog. 'Does this film have a significance for me?' I ask him. 'Yes, yes. You must realise that the truth is in you and you must follow the yellow brick road. Look around,' he tells me. Now we are on the yellow brick road, now I am dressed up as Dorothy, wearing her outfit. There are flowers all around us. I now look at my teacher and he looks like my uncle who died 15 years ago. He tells me, 'Help your father, he needs help. He needs to express himself but he can't. Now go away, you need to help him. Go speak to him, you could help him. You can't let this happen to him, you must talk to him. He can't live the way he is living.' We are in a cave, and its light and my uncle has a map behind him. He looks like a professor and he is writing something on a chalkboard: TALK TO HIM. 'Now go,' he tells me, 'you're dismissed.' I go back with Tiki and we are in my power place, where I used to live while I was in university. There are parties going on around us. My uncle appears again. 'All of this must stop; this excitement, you must learn to focus on what's important. This will all be there in the future, he won't. So you must speak to him. I must go.' Tiki asks me, 'Did you understand what happened? You must use your brain and open up and feel and speak the truth and not let anyone intimidate you.' We walk down the stairs and down the street. There is an old carriage with a man sitting on it circling around us and then it turns and goes off, goes away. I say goodbye to Tiki and he sails away. I am back from the journey. The significant message I had from the journey is not to be intimidated to open up and speak to people, and the limelight will always be there, but speak to people I need to speak to now.

This journey is an example of how a single journey to the upper world may have great transformative effects on a person's life. When I asked Dian how the journey had impacted on her life, she wrote:

This was my third journey and the most powerful journey of all. Through my first two journeys I came to acknowledge that I had a problem with communication. This was hard for me to imagine, since in college I had studied communication, I wanted to pursue a career in communication, and I had always believed that I was the best communicator in the world. But in reality, deep down I knew that I could never really communicate my true thoughts and feelings. The journey literally opened my eyes. I was shocked to see the problems in my life which I needed to deal with, but was not, due to my lack of communicating my true feelings. One encounter which was especially significant for me was meeting my uncle, who had died when I was a child. Although I didn't know him well, his death impacted on my life greatly, since for me it was the first experience of death in my family. My uncle was telling me that I must talk with my father, which surprised me at the time, since I thought my father was perfectly fine. It was only later that I found out that at the time I did the journey he was headed towards a rough time in his life, and perhaps even death. Another significant message that impacted on me was related to a scene of my college days, which was a carefree time in my life. I realised that in my heart I wanted to return to those days, and that wanting to do so was because I didn't wish to grow up. The journey taught me that it was time to move on and take responsibility for my life. There were a lot of emotions in this journey which I had bottled up my entire life, and were now coming up. Following this journey I am more able to express myself freely and am not ashamed to admit to my feelings. Although it was very difficult for me to understand the meaning of this journey at the time, as time passed I came to understand the messages behind it. Although I have to admit that there are times when I suppress my true thoughts and emotions, I am learning to take it day by day and make the changes needed to complete my life one step at a time.

MIDDLE WORLD JOURNEYS

The middle world traversed by the shaman is in fact our own familiar world as perceived by them while in an ASC. Middle world journeys are used for dealing with mundane issues, and for receiving practical advice and help. Among shamanic cultures, the purpose of journeying to this realm is usually to gather information regarding weather, hunting, fishing or possible conflicts with neighbouring tribes. The shaman goes on a journey to the middle world, sweeping over great distances of land to locate migrating herds of animals, check weather conditions or possible dangers from neighbouring tribes or the elements. Middle world journeys are more common among the Siberian and North American tribes, perhaps due to scarcity of food supplies in those areas.[14]

Today, in the West, we don't have the lifestyle that would require us to search for migrating buffalo herds. However, we have plenty of other mundane and practical issues we may wish to deal with, and for those purposes the middle world journey is ideal. People might have problems with their bosses or colleagues at their workplace, quarrel or have unresolved issues with friends and family members. It is important to acknowledge that mundane issues are not unimportant, but rather that they are issues which have to do with the ordinary, daily aspects of our lives. For example, a woman I once worked with was going through an acrimonious divorce. She and her husband had sold their house but he was delaying the signing of papers that would release the money from the sale. In the meantime she had bought a new house and was paying a very high rate mortgage interest on it. She was desperate to receive the money but her husband was persistently avoiding signing the papers. She did a journey to the middle world and spoke to her husband's soul. After returning from the journey she told me she felt that in her journey they had both spoken all that had been left unspoken between them and that she now felt at peace with him. The next day she opened her email to find a letter from her husband, informing her that he had signed the papers and sent them to the lawyer.

Middle world journeys are ideal for times when we wish to observe and understand our lives, or some other aspect of our immediate reality. These journeys help us to gain a more in-depth understanding of our lives, our selves and of others. We might say that while journeying to the middle world we distance ourselves from our daily situation, and look at it from an altered state of consciousness or a different perspective. This allows us to see the situation through the eyes of our souls, without the interference of the ego and our mind. We are then able to see the truth without judgement.

It's important to be aware, however, that middle world journeys are not out of body experiences. As mentioned before, one of the key elements characterising the shamanic journey is the element of journeying at will. Out of body experiences, although sometimes similar to shamanic middle world journeys in terms of content, are not taken voluntarily, but rather, spontaneously.

Meeting the soul of a living person

One of the most magical middle world journeys we can make is the journey to meet the soul of a living person. This journey is taken with the purpose of healing a relationship with a person in our life that we may have conflict with. To accomplish this, we travel to the middle world to meet the soul of the person we are having the difficulty with, with the intention of communicating on a soul level with that person, hearing them and being heard by them.

It is very important that our intention should not be to fight, blame or force that person to see things our way. Rather, the point is to come to have clear communication with that person, a communication that is not hindered by our emotions and mind. Sometimes we can also ask for a spirit teacher to help and support us, or intervene whenever necessary. This is a very powerful journey. During the years that I have been involved in shamanic work, I have always experienced it to be effective and fruitful.

One example that comes to my mind is that of an Argentinian woman who attended my shamanic course for beginners. This woman journeyed very well and appeared to be at ease with her spirit teachers. She had no problem entering an altered state of consciousness and communicating with her spirits. Towards the end of the course she approached me and shared with me an issue relating to her relationship with her daughter, that was troubling her very much. She told me that six months ago, her daughter had left the family home and severed all contact with all the family members.

They knew that she was still living in the country, but had no idea where.

Knowing that she could journey well and that she had formed a relationship with her spirit teachers, I asked her if she felt ready and comfortable to do a middle world journey and meet the soul of her daughter. She was very happy to try and do that. Her journey was a true revelation to her. When she came back, her first words to me were, 'My God, I really don't know my daughter!' She had realised how little she had truly listened to her daughter in the past. It was only in the journey that she felt that for the first time she was gaining a deeper understanding of their relationship and the conflict that they were having. The day after the course I received a phone call, around lunchtime. The woman was crying with joy and told me that that very night, after the course, she had received a phone call from her daughter, and that they had agreed to meet that afternoon for coffee and a talk.

Although the communication in this sort of journey is done on a soul level, it is very important that the person does not go on the journey with judgement, anger, wanting revenge or with blaming. If we embark on this journey with an agenda in the back on our minds, the communication with the other person's soul will not happen and we will not achieve the results we seek.

Another important point regarding this sort of journey is that the results we may receive from it are varied. We won't necessarily receive a phone call or renew a dying relationship following the journey. However, assuming that we have not journeyed with an agenda, a resolution of some sort should happen. I experienced myself a painful break-up of a friendship a few years ago. I embarked on a middle world journey to speak to the soul of my friend. Although she did not call me or write to me following the journey, something had changed in me. When I thought about my friend, the sadness, the confusion, the intense emotions, were no longer there. I felt at peace with that relationship and with that person. Before, when I thought of her, I would feel a great sense of loss, pain and hurt. After the journey these feelings no longer had a hold over me. I could only feel peace and love thinking of her.

When we interact with the soul of the person that we journey to and meet in the middle world, we are actually interacting with the soul or the spiritual aspect of that person. The other person does not have to be consciously aware of what happened during the journey, or even that the journey occurred. However, if their soul is willing to interact with our own, the changes in the relationship miraculously happen.

Journey through the eyes of our guardian spirit

Another powerful journey which we can make to the middle world is a journey to observe a situation in our lives through the eyes of our guardian spirit. At times we are too involved and too close to issues that are strongly affecting our lives and we cannot see the wood for the trees. In this sort of journey the person asks their guardian spirit for help in seeing the particular situation or state in their lives through the guardian's eyes. The journey begins with the person literally entering the guardian spirit and completely merging with it.

The experiences people have on such journeys are extremely varied, but they always receive a new and enlightening perspective on their presenting problem. This kind of journey could be seen, in psychological terms, to be using a form of dissociation. Distancing ourselves from the situation and observing it from another perspective (the guardian spirit's eyes) may grant us clearer vision and understanding of where we stand. In shamanic terms, however, the power of this journey is not credited to dissociation, but rather to the fact that we are observing the situation through the wise eyes of our guardian spirit.

SPONTANEOUS JOURNEYS

While shamans spend considerable time and effort developing their journeying skills, journey-like experiences may occur frequently and spontaneously among people with no shamanic aspirations whatsoever. Two such forms of journey-like experiences are near-death experiences and out of body experiences, in which people experience themselves or their soul leaving their physical body and travelling. Many people report that these experiences have enriched their lives and given them deep insight.

However, journey-like experiences are even more common than we might think. We have all experienced dreams where we have been to strange places we have never visited in our ordinary reality. Most of us have dreamt about dead people, and sometimes we have experienced dreams with wonderful scenery. All of these experiences appear totally real to us while dreaming. In shamanic cultures dreams are likened to journeying – it is believed that while we are dreaming our soul travels to the spirit world. Thus, dreams are valued as insightful experiences among people of shamanic cultures. Many religions, spiritual practices and psychologies also hold the belief that dreams can provide us with deep insights and new understandings of our lives.

A specific type of dream that is even more similar to the shamanic journey is the lucid dream. Lucid dreams are dreams in which the dreamer is aware of the fact that they are dreaming and is able to willingly direct the course of the dream to some extent. This form of dreaming has actually been used for centuries by Buddhists as a way of acquiring wisdom. All of these experiences could be considered as spontaneous journeys.

We can conclude from this that journey-like experiences are universal. Additionally, if we are all capable of having these experiences and they occur spontaneously in people, we might be able to conclude that the ability to journey is innate to human beings. This could further be used to provide support to a claim made by many: that shamanism did not spread around the world through migration, but rather it naturally and spontaneously developed in all human societies. If journey-like experiences are innate to all human beings, and happen spontaneously, these very experiences could have led people into developing their journeying abilities consciously, leading to the birth of shamanic practices. This, then, could provide an explanation as to how shamanism came to exist all over the world, as well as explain the similarities existing between different shamanic cultures, and the reason these practices have survived to date.

CORE SHAMANISM

Can westerners journey shamanically?

The question arises whether shamanic journeys can be undertaken successfully and effectively by contemporary westerners lacking any traditional shamanic cultural background and education. The answer given by Michael Harner[15] to this question is a definite 'yes'. He reports that among modern westerners approximately nine out of ten people can journey successfully. From my experience of working shamanically, I have come to notice that almost everybody succeeds in journeying, although initially the depth and intensity of the journeys as well as the depth of understanding of them varies from person to person. Most westerners today can and do journey at will to the spirit world to seek healing and knowledge, very much like the shamans of old.

However, it is important for us to note that there is a difference between journeying shamanically (shamanising) and being an actual shaman. In many different shamanic cultures, community members, at times, journey to the spirit world by themselves, unassisted by the shaman. Among the North American Indians, every single person may journey and each has a guardian spirit, obtained by the same means that the shaman acquires their own spirit helpers. The difference between the shaman and the layman is considered to be merely quantitative; the shaman has more spirit teachers and embodies greater shamanic power. In this respect, Eliade[16] claims, every Native American could be said to 'shamanise' although they do not have any aspirations to become shamans.

Another significant difference between shamanising and practising as a shaman relates to the issue of responsibility. While every person may shamanise and journey for themselves, only the shaman holds responsibility for the health of the entire community. The role of the shaman entails in it a great deal of responsibility and hardships and requires extensive training, experience and skills. As discussed in the previous chapter, the shaman often goes through an initiatory crisis or illness followed by many years apprenticeship to an experienced shaman as well as to the spirits before starting to serve their community. This applies, of course, to the work of core shamanism as practised today. I believe it is important for people who undertake core shamanism courses and training to bear in mind that there is a great difference between practising shamanism for ourselves and being a shamanic counsellor. One cannot become a shaman or shamanic counsellor by participating in a core shamanism weekend workshop, or by reading a DIY book on shamanism.

Shamanic counselling

Shamanic counselling is a method for healing which draws on the principles of classic shamanic practices. The method was developed initially and primarily by Michael Harner, who was the first to introduce shamanism back into the therapeutic sphere in the West. While shamanic counselling draws on both modern and ancient traditions of healing, it is distinctly different from both traditional shamanic practices and modern therapeutic ones.

While in traditional shamanic cultures it is the shaman who usually journeys to the spirit world on behalf of the ill person, in shamanic counselling the emphasis is reversed. It is the person who is in need of help that does most of the journeying and shamanic work, directly contacting their spirit teachers. That is mainly due to the fact that the emphasis in shamanic counselling practices is on self-empowerment and self-healing. However, certain aspects of the shaman's traditional work are still alive in the practice of shamanic counselling. When a soul retrieval, power animal retrieval, certain healing or diagnostic work is necessary, the counsellor would assume the traditional role of the shaman and perform a journey on behalf of the person seeking help. We will explore these methods of shamanic healing later on in Chapter5.

One of the most debated questions regarding shamanic counselling, and indeed shamanic practices as a whole, is whether or not they could be regarded as a type of psychotherapy. This is a valid question since many similarities exist between psychotherapy and shamanic practices. Jerome Frank, one of the main psychotherapy researchers, recounts the basic characteristics of psychotherapy:

Psychotherapy is a planned, emotionally charged, confiding interaction between a trained, socially sanctioned healer and a sufferer. During this interaction the healer seeks to relieve the sufferer's distress and disability through symbolic communications, primarily words but also sometimes bodily activities. The healer may or may not involve the patient's relatives and others in the healing rituals.[17]

It is clear from this definition how shamanic healing may be perceived to be a form of psychotherapy, since Frank's definition could easily be applied to it as well. It could be said that many of the techniques used by shamans throughout the globe are extremely similar to psychotherapeutic techniques. In fact, many claim that the effectiveness of shamanic interventions is based on psychological mechanisms. We shall discuss this issue at length later on in Chapter 6, but for now it is worth noting that certain similarities do seem to exist between shamanic work and psychotherapy. However, I believe that, at the end of the day, shamanic practices differ considerably from western therapies. That is mainly due to the role played by the shamanic counsellor. While a relationship does form between the counsellor and the person seeking help, and the nature of this relationship bears on the healing process, the role of the counsellor is more that of a facilitator rather than a therapist. Put simply, the counsellor's job is mainly to help the person come into direct contact with their own spirit helpers. In this way, the person receives their teachings and healing directly from their spirits and not indirectly via the counsellor. This is one of the most empowering and important elements of shamanic counselling and also serves to filter out the assumptions and biases of the therapist (such as transference and counter-transference) which may influence the therapeutic process. The shamanic counsellor fulfils several important roles in facilitating the person's successful and fruitful encounter with the spirit world. The main task of the counsellor is to help the client gain clarity regarding what help they wish to receive from the spirits and formulate the correct mission in order to achieve that. Another role of the counsellor is to explain to the person how to enter non-ordinary reality in order to journey as well as how to operate and communicate effectively within the realms of the spirits.

When the person returns from the journey it is important that the counsellor does not actually advise or interpret the meaning of any symbols or metaphors contained in the journey. Although such metaphors and symbols are discussed in the session afterwards, it is the counsellor's role to bring the person to a point where they are able to interpret and intuit meaning for themselves. Although suggestions can be made by the counsellor, the main emphasis in shamanic counselling is upon the person's own understanding of the journey. The overriding theory behind this is that the best qualified person to understand such information is the journeyer themselves. Thus, the power of the shamanic counselling process lies in the fact that it frees the person from dependency on the therapist and directs them towards their own self-empowerment.

While it is clear that the base of power and knowledge is not within the counsellor, it is equally important for the counsellor to prevent the person seeking help from becoming overly dependent on their own spirit teachers, and end up journeying excessively. Some people tend to transfer their dependency habit from the human counsellor to the spirits. This results in them wanting to journey and ask the spirits for advice and help on every little thing in their lives. They become, in effect, what my teacher Jonathan refers to as 'journey-junkies'.

The fact is that it does not require many shamanic journeys to bring about transformation in our lives. This is where the journeyer's *intention* comes to play a role in the healing. If we allow ourselves to be open and truly listen to the messages of the spirits, and consequently put them into action in our lives, we will not require many journeys to support us in our process of transformation. In fact, I have worked with many people who experienced a profound change in their lives following a single journey.

As to the question whether shamanic counselling is psychotherapy or not, I would answer that it is not. However, I do believe that shamanic counselling is a form of therapeutic intervention. The shaman is concerned, first and foremost, in relieving suffering and pain, in promoting health, equilibrium and healing. All therapies bring about healing of a sort. Thus I consider shamanic practices and shamanic counselling to be a form of therapy. The therapy of the shaman, however, is a much older one than that of modern psychology, and is considerably different. Although I believe it is wrong to refer to shamanism as psychotherapy, I also strongly believe that it is the great ancestor of our modern-age therapies.

SHAMANIC RITUALS

As mentioned before, the whole journey process is comprised of more than just the journey proper. The preparation for the journey as well as the rituals performed following it are just as important to the process of journeying. Just as the indigenous shaman goes through the three stages of the journey – preparation, journeying and return – so do western practitioners of core shamanism today. Let us explore some of the rituals performed by practitioners of core shamanism.

The power of ritual

Ritual is essential to human beings. No matter in which culture, we find rituals wherever we look, pervading every level of our lives. Jean Piaget,[18] one of the forefathers of child developmental psychology, pointed to the fact that commonplace, mundane rituals, related to dressing, eating and sleeping start playing a central role in children around the age of three. Children as young as three years old start employing ritualistic behaviours in an attempt to learn how life is structured. Socialised ritual or ceremony make an appearance later on in life.

Although we might initially associate the concept of ritual with faraway cultures where young men of an Amazonian tribe endure pain and are exposed to dangers as part of their rites of passage into manhood, the fact is that we need not look so far; ritual is highly prevalent in our own lives. We all experience rituals – from the mundane rituals we 'religiously' perform every morning (like brushing our teeth or drinking coffee) through the different kinds of rites of passage we all had to go through as we navigated through life (such as our graduation ceremony from university, or a bar mitzvah celebration). Ritual never leaves our lives; it just changes its form.

Many theories have been proposed to explain rituals, their nature and functions. Like any other complex social phenomenon, it is possible to address and understand rituals from multiple perspectives. Thus, I do not propose to provide here a single definition of ritual, nor do I attempt to include within my definition the entire spectrum of functions that might be fulfilled by rituals in our daily lives.

I believe that all rituals, from the mundane to the sacred, from the ones performed in modern industrial societies to those of the indigenous villages in South America, all share similar functions. Or rather, all rituals bring about two general results. First, rituals serve to create a frame and a structure and second, they function to bring about a transition from one state of consciousness to another.

Rituals relating to shamanic practices are many and varied, their symbology and nature depending on the culture in question. As mentioned before, the traditional shaman undergoes special rituals and preparations before and after journeying. Just like the indigenous shaman, a core shamanic practitioner also undergoes specific rituals prior to and following a journey. One of the functions of these rituals is to create sameness and repetitiveness which puts us at ease and allows us to let go of our mind.

However, a more important function fulfilled by shamanic rituals is creating a change in our state of consciousness. It is the performance of the ritual which begins the transition from our daily ordinary state of consciousness into the shamanic state of consciousness, preparing us for contact with the spirit world. The ritual, almost literally, creates a different reality around us, thus helping us to slip into a different state of being. In short, the shamanic ritual is primarily *a catalyst for change*.

In the following section I introduce some of the shamanic rituals performed by practitioners of core shamanism before and after going on a journey. There is no doubt, however, that many other rituals which are commonly used today by people in order to enter a shamanic state of consciousness will be missing. That is not because they are less important or less powerful, but rather because I am less familiar with them in my daily practice. However, it is important to remember that it is not the particularities of a certain ritual which make it powerful, but rather its meaning, lurking behind the specific actions, words or tools we use. Most symbols and rituals are culturally determined and constructed to meet the needs of each particular population or even each particular person, and yet they are all effective. It is not the specifics of the ritual itself which bring about change or healing. It is the power that one gives to the ritual which makes it so effective.

Pre-journey rituals

Mental preparation

The first stage of preparation prior to journeying starts roughly one to two hours before the actual journey takes place. The journeyer begins by mentally preparing themselves for the work at hand. In the case of journeying for somebody else, the journeyer would begin to think of the person and the work or mission that needs to be carried out. In the case of journeying for oneself, the mental preparation is focused on the mission or merely on the prospect of venturing into the realms of the spirits. The next step is listening to a slow rhythmic drumming sound. While listening to the drum additional rituals are carried out, such as cleaning the room, the equipment and self with sage, incense or other herbs, lighting a candle and preparing the room for the journey. Some people may also have specific personal rituals given to them by their own spirit helpers for this purpose.

The purpose of this is to separate oneself from ordinary reality and to mentally prepare to enter a different state of consciousness; leaving one consciousness behind to enter the other. We accomplish this on several levels, using mental functions, auditory, visual and other sensory aids. The purification of the room, the equipment and the journeyer by burning sage, incense or other herbs also helps to energetically clean the shamanic paraphernalia and surroundings before the journey. This purification ritual also serves to focus the attention on the work at hand and mentally let go of the mind, leaving behind any daily concerns.

Rattling

The rattle is one of the instruments most universally used by shamans to call upon the spirits, and it is the first tool used by every core shamanism practitioner when embarking on a journey. The rattle, just like the drum, is another powerful instrument which helps the shaman to enter an altered state of consciousness. It helps one to exceed one's boundaries and let go of the mind, or in Don Juan's words, it helps one in 'losing self-importance'. It is through this process that a marked shift to a shamanic state of consciousness begins. Rattling before journeying marks the initial contact with the spirit helpers.

Just as the drum is considered by some cultures to be made from the world tree, in the case of the rattle it is the handle which represents the tree and the hollow gourd which is thought to represent the universe. The stones or seeds to be found inside the rattle are the spirits and souls of the shaman's ancestors. By shaking the rattle, the shaman invokes the power of these powerful spirit allies.

The specifics of the rattling ritual vary from culture to culture and from practitioner to practitioner. I present here one of the more common versions of a rattling ritual prior to journeying, used by many core shamanism practitioners.

The aim of the basic rattling ritual performed before a journey is to invite the spirits of the cardinal corners – the north, south, east and west – to join the shaman or journeyer. The call is also to invite the spirits of the upper world, lower world and middle world, or any helping spirits that could offer their help to the journeyer. This process is done by facing in each direction and shaking the rattle four times, inviting the spirits of that direction and asking for their help. This is done repeatedly with each direction. For example, one would be facing the east, rattle four times and ask the spirits of that direction to join you, while continuing rattling. This would then be repeated, facing the south, the west and the north, the upper, lower and middle worlds. After this initial call to the spirits, rattling continues freely, while the person interacts with their spirit helpers through dancing, singing, or other rituals given to them by those helpers specifically for this purpose. The rattling process could actually mark the beginning of the journey, and the person might receive significant messages or images before even starting the actual journey.

The rattling ritual, the specific directions and the order by which they are addressed, vary from person to person. I start in the east and then go sun-wise. Others may start with the east and face the north next, and so on. The actual ritual following the initial calling of the spirits also varies considerably. For me, often, the spirit of my rattle joins me immediately, and we dance together. He may have messages for me – either personal, or messages regarding the work I am going to embark on. I also have other personal rituals that have been given to me by my spirit teachers and which I have been instructed to keep secret.

The rattle, for me, acts as a telephone to the spirit world, or as my teacher Jonathan once explained, 'I often call the rattle a *power antenna*. Sometimes when I'm standing and calling the spirits, I feel like a man holding onto a lightning rod as I feel the power flowing through me.' The significance of the rattle is not the tool itself, but rather the spirits which reside within it. Thus, it is very important that we do not try to control our rattle or direct its movements, but allow ourselves to listen to the spirits of the rattle and feel the flow of their power, allowing them to guide the rattling. It is important to become friends with your rattle. Just as we can ride on the sound of the drum, we can fly on the wings of the rattle.

The rattle has many other important uses in shamanic work. It has great healing power and can be used for diagnostic purposes, to diagnose and treat physical, psychological or spiritual blockages. The healing uses of the rattle will be explored more fully in Chapter 5.

Creating darkness and stating the mission

The next stage in the preparation for journeying is the darkening of the room, covering the eyes in order to create full darkness, followed by stating the mission of the journey four times. These rituals are performed immediately before actually journeying and going into a full ASC, by listening to a monotonous drum beat (either on tape or live). Most core shamanism practitioners state the mission of the journey twice before drumming commences and twice with the sound of the drums.

Traditionally, among shamanic cultures, journeys take place either at night or at twilight, with the shaman's eyes closed or half closed. One reason could be that we are able to see images much more vividly in conditions of darkness. Not only that, but in that state our attention is not distracted as much by visual stimulation from our surroundings and we are able to slip more easily into an ASC. In the darkness, we can see the spirits better.

Among the Alaskan Inuit, a person aspiring to become a shaman might approach an older shaman with the request, 'I come to you because I desire to see.' The idea of inner sight as a source of wisdom is quite widespread in many shamanic cultures. Thus, the loss of a person's natural eyesight may mark them as having been chosen by the spirits to become a shaman. This concept is to be found also in non shamanic cultures, as well as in Greek mythology. Tiresias, after being struck blind by the goddess Hera, was gifted with second sight by Zeus.

Special sight is considered in many cultures to be one of the shaman's most important tools or strengths. The Siberian shaman of the Avam Samoyed, Huottarie, had his eyes gouged out by a spirit on his initiatory journey, to be replaced with new eyes, especially adapted to see other realities.[19] When we journey, we cover our eyes so that our inner eyes might be opened and we are able to see beyond this world and into the world of the spirits.

The mission

When journeying to the spirit world, having a clear purpose is very important. Performing all the preparatory rituals aids us to enter an altered state of consciousness more easily and establish initial contact with our spirit helpers. Stating the mission four times helps our mind to focus on the reason we are journeying.

This is true especially for westerners who are less experienced at journeying and have greater difficulty in letting go of their conscious mind. That is why it is not enough to just think of the mission or state it only once, but four times. The intention we have while going on a journey is one of the key components for the success of the journey, and for us getting results.

Having a mission puts the journeyer on the right road and keeps them in contact with the purpose of their journey. Thus, while journeying and interacting with their spirit teachers, they are able to focus better on the questions that they need to ask and the information they seek. Saying the mission four times at the beginning of the journey gives us clarity on both conscious and unconscious levels. Being clear about our purpose, we are also capable of letting go and allowing ourselves to remain in an altered state of consciousness, being more present in the spirit world.

Post-journey rituals

Returning from the journey, one would either write it down or listen to the words of the journey as recorded. In both cases, we would be going over the journey and attempting to make sense of the symbolism and messages contained in it, especially in relation to the mission. This is important because by doing this we are introducing these new messages into our daily life. By trying to understand the symbols and messages of our journey, we are deepening the effects which have already taken place on a deeper level of our consciousness.

If a tape is used, it remains important to have a full written account of the journey. Reading the journey periodically is highly recommended. When reading the same journey at different periods of time, most people report gaining significant new understandings of the symbols and messages contained therein. It is also important for the person to try and notice or be aware of the manner in which the journey has affected their lives – how or whether they are experiencing the desired outcomes.

Other than the above rituals, which are carried out after every single journey, it is also possible that the journeyer receives instructions to perform certain specific rituals for a certain period of time after returning. These are healing or therapeutic rituals which the person may be instructed to carry out as part of their process of healing. One example which stands out in my mind is that of a woman I once worked with.

Shira had lost her second husband to cancer only three months following his initial diagnosis. This was a great and terrible shock for her. She and her husband had been building a new house for a long time and were expecting to move into it. Tragically, she ended up moving to her new home one week after the death of her husband. Although she was functioning in her daily life, emotionally Shira was experiencing great difficulties.

She had no knowledge of shamanism, but based on prior acquaintance with me, decided, two months following her husband's death, to seek help from the spirits. I went on a diagnostic journey to enquire what help Shira needed at that time in her life. Other than the many direct teachings and messages she received in the journey, my teacher also said that although it is natural to grieve she need not indulge in her grieving and, to my surprise, instructed her to carry out a daily ritual. For a period of a month she was to take a candle and a red rose to her husband's grave every morning. She was then to light the candle, leave the rose in a vase on the grave, sit still for a while and go home, leaving the candle burning. The day after she was to repeat the ritual and at the end of it take the old rose home with her. At the end of the month she was to take the accumulated thirty roses, walk to the sea and stand on top of a cliff. She was then to take all the dried rose petals in her hands, crumble them and blow them into the wind.

This ritual was a powerful healing experience for Shira and spoke to her very strongly. She later said that although the ritual was embarrassing and difficult to carry out at times, she nevertheless carried it out automatically and 'religiously'. She felt it obliged her to stay with the grieving and the pain over the loss of her husband, rather than escaping it, which was her natural tendency. The ritual, she explained, made both her husband's death and the grieving process more real.

The symbology of the ritual also spoke to her greatly. Collecting the flowers, lighting a candle on the grave and eventually blowing the flowers over the sea touched her. But most of all, she felt the ritual provided her with the sense that her grieving had its place. It had a beginning, but also an end. The ritual allowed her to both feel her grief as well as eventually let go of it. This also connected Shira with one of the direct messages given by the teacher in the journey, that she was not to indulge in the grieving. She felt the ritual helped her to do just that.

In other cases, of either a soul retrieval or power animal retrieval, the shaman might receive instructions from the spirits to pass on to the person receiving the help about rituals the person must perform in order to embody the soul or power animal. This process is fully explained in Chapter 5.

* * *

I went to look for the place from which I would go on my vision quest. I came to a lake with two large boulders near its bank. The mountains were in front of me.

I touched the rock. 'You are so warm.'

'I am you.'

I touched it again and it felt soft like velvet. 'You are so strong and yet so soft.'

'I am you.'

'You have the shape of a heart to me . . .'

'Yes, you are home.'

I began to question my choice. Did this place really call me, or was it just my imagination? After all, I had not gone very far to find it.

'You don't have to search far, or travel far, to be in your heart. To be in your heart, where your home is. No matter how far you travel, the journey to your heart, your home, is a short one.'

Eventually, I began to walk away, still questioning my choice of place, but no matter where I went or how long I searched, the rocks back by the lake were calling me. When I came back and looked at them from a distance, one looked like a crocodile and the other one the shape of a ram, facing each other, talking. And I suddenly noticed an opening between them, like a window, a window which was shaped like a heart.

'Yes, look at things through the eye of your heart,' I heard the rock telling me.

'What is the meaning of the animals?' I asked

'You will know in time. When you learn to look through the window of your heart.'

I then looked at the lake, it was so calm and the ducks were swimming, very calmly.

I heard, 'Arvick, they don't worry about whether there will be water in the lake tomorrow. They are just enjoying the moment; not even the day, but just the moment.'

Here and on the following pages are pieces of artwork produced by participants on a shamanic course. The significant messages of the journeys undertaken were drawn on the canvas so that each complete image tells the progressive story of participant's lessons and experiences during the entire course.

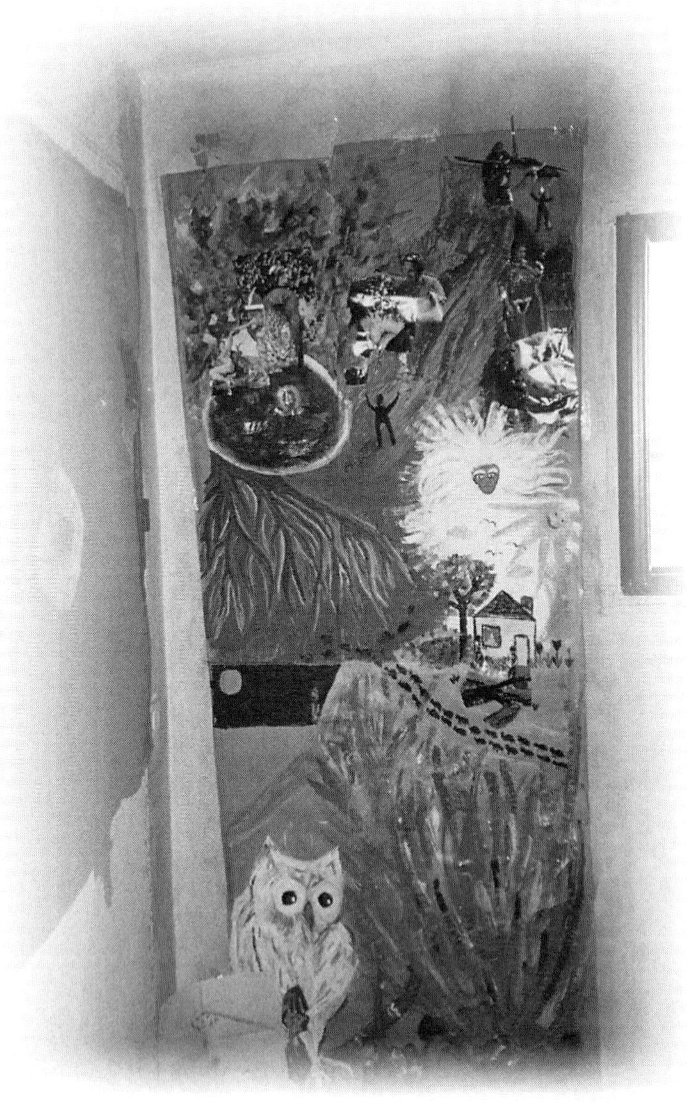

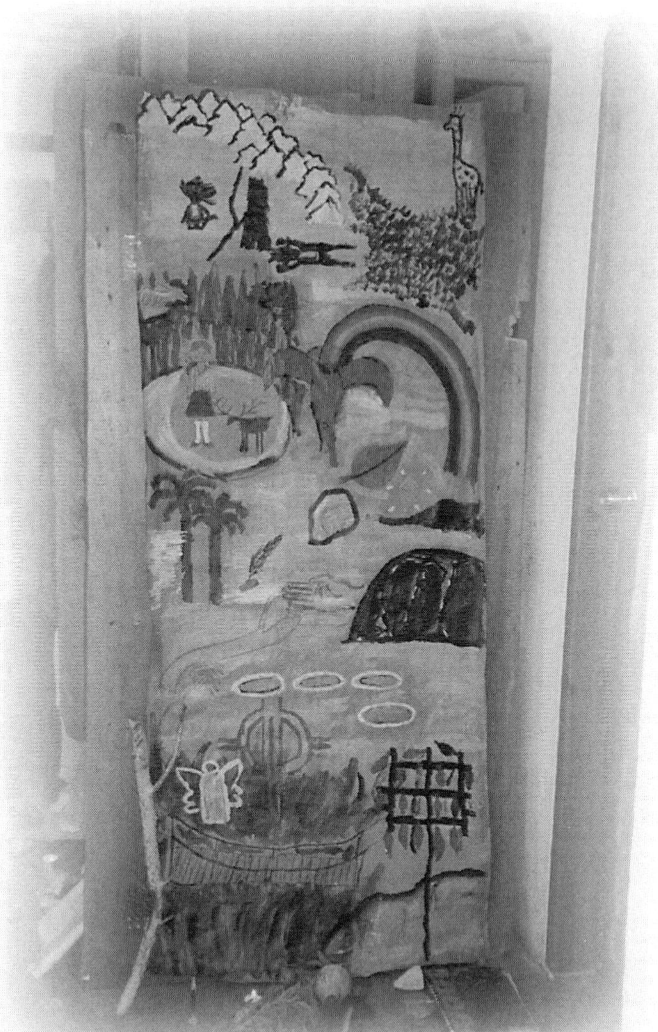

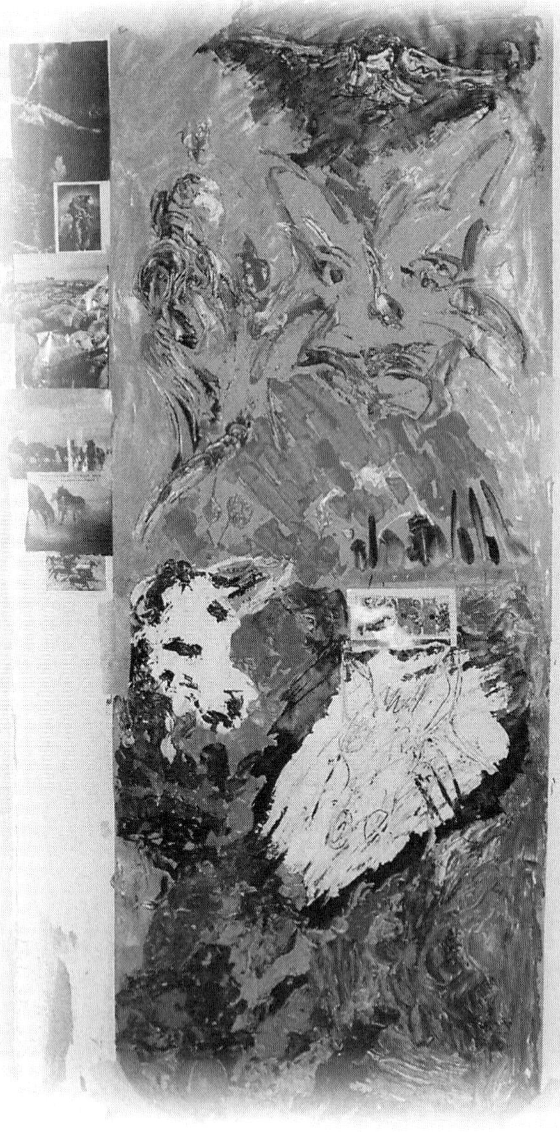

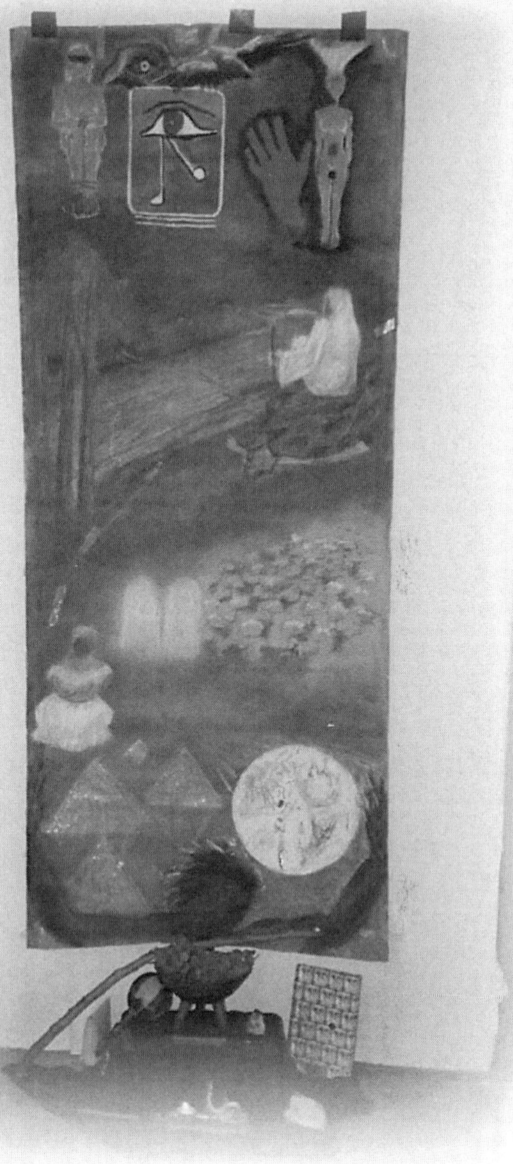

4 *Beyond the Ego: Spirits and Spirituality*

*We are the keys to different doors,
and different windows in your mind.*
Spirit teacher

I was seven. My father was working away from home, as always. He was a chef and there was not much work for him in Isfahan, where we lived. So he used to work away for long periods of time and visit us briefly in between, though he was very regular with sending money and taking care of my mother and me. My father sacrificed a lot for us. I was his only child and he endured the separation from both my mother and me so that he would be able to provide for us. A few months following his last visit, we lost contact with him. We did not know where he was. The last news we had of him, he was working as a chef for the Russians in Tehran. I remember this as one of the most difficult periods in our lives.

My mother had three brothers. One lived in the south of Iran and the other two lived in Isfahan, my place of birth. She was the sister and she took them under her wing and they decided to live together since my father was away most of the time. My father was a good provider and there was always plenty in our home. Money was flowing in. We were well off. The oldest of my uncles was engaged to be married and the wedding was being delayed by his fiancée. Eventually, one day, he told my mother that his fiancée had said, 'I will marry you only if you live separately from your sister.' So he suggested that my mother temporarily take me and go and live somewhere else. At that time, as it happened, a few months later we lost contact with my father. Too proud to ask for help, one day my mother realised that she had no money to even buy bread for the day after.

The room where we were living was small, almost like a cellar, with steps into the ground. It was on the far corner of a huge garden house. The centre of the yard was an orchard with vines and apples and all sorts of fruit trees. It had a huge wooden gate, strong and old-fashioned, with a heavy knocker. That night, realising that she had no money and didn't know how she would provide food for me, my mother prayed to her surp-hoki, or holy spirits. She prayed asking for help. At four o'clock in the morning, from the depths of the yard, in her sleep, she heard someone knocking at the gate. Wondering who it could be, and since no one answered and the knocking continued, she went out to the gate. She opened the door and there was no one there, but there were ten tooman, laid on the platform by the side of the gate. In those days, most houses in Iran had big wooden gates with two large platforms built either side. In cool evenings, people would usually sit on the platforms to talk and share food. As ten tooman was a large sum of money those days, my mother called out to the darkness, asking if anyone was there. There was no answer, and she was frightened, but since there was no one there, she took the money and came back. That kept us for ten days. And then, miraculously, we heard from my father, and money started arriving again. My mother always told me, whenever you are in trouble, stuck or need advice, all you have to do is talk to your surp-hoki.

SPIRIT HELPERS

In order to understand shamanism, we must understand the shaman's world. We have explored the cosmology, practices and worldviews of shamans. As we learned, the shaman's universe is teeming with life and spirits. And it is the spirits who are the key players in shamanic cultures, and thus in our story. Without the spirits there would be no shaman. But what are spirits? On one of the journeys I made asking for guidance in the writing of this book, my guardian spirit told me:

> *'In this work, it's the spirits that are the key characters, the key players, Arvick. You come to the spirits to get help, so it's us you need to write about. We are all keys that open different doors, and different windows in your mind, to help you penetrate deeper. And to be able to help yourselves, to be happy. We are there for anyone that wants to take responsibility for their health and happiness. We do not discriminate.'*

When we look at different shamanic cultures around the world, we can see that spirits reveal themselves in a multitude of forms. These forms are often grounded in the myths, beliefs and stories of the culture that the shaman or journeyer is part of. For the Native American shaman the spirits may appear in the forms of animals with special cultural significance, such as bears, eagles or wolves, while the spirit teachers of the Japanese shaman, on the other hand, may take the form of a transformation of the Buddha.

From my experience, spirits may take not only the shape of humans or animals, but also of plants, celestial bodies or even abstract forms such as colours and lights. A woman I worked with, for instance, had a small violet flower as her guardian spirit, and one man who attended one of my workshops had the sun as one of his spirit teachers. However, we do not directly perceive the true form or essence of spirits. I believe that spirits are essentially bundles of light or energy, and that they present themselves to us in forms which are familiar or understandable to us. To put this in Jungian terms, we may all share the same archetypes, but they manifest themselves in our lives through different specific forms that are understandable to us.

Shamans usually establish a relationship with several helping spirits in addition to their guardian spirit. The number of these spirits varies from shaman to shaman and from culture to culture. In certain cultures, such as the native tribes of Alaska, the more helping spirits the shaman has contact with the more powerful the shaman is. A shaman requires several years to assemble a large enough crew of spirit helpers, who help them carry out their healing work. This requires years of practice, work and dedication, during which they strive to form relationships with their spirit helpers and traverse the spirit world with confidence and trust.

Spirits not only come in different shapes and forms, but also possess different qualities and serve different purposes for the shaman. The reason the shaman needs several spirits is because they are not all the same! Each spirit serves and helps the shaman with a different aspect of their healing work.

For example, in my case, when I initially started to work shamanically, for a few years I had only my guardian spirit and one spirit teacher. Gradually, I acquired teachers for specific work. Some of my spirits are mainly there to transport me to different levels of the spirit worlds. These spirits appear in forms of mythical animals and angels. I have spirit helpers who are teachers and other spirits who are healers. I have a teacher that deals with psychological issues, and a teacher that appears whenever the person I am working with has suffered severe childhood trauma. One particular teacher always appears whenever the person I am working with has issues related to religion and religious belief systems that are affecting their lives.

I have healers that accompany me on specific shamanic works – such as my teacher for soul retrieval, and my teacher for healing who instructs me and guides me on various healing journeys. Some of my other healers have human form and some have animal form. My shamanic tools also have spirits– the spirit of the rattle and the drum, that guide and support me whenever I am using either of these tools. Finally, there are spirits who are the helpers of my healing teacher and advise me on the various medicinal aspects of my work.

WHAT ARE SPIRITS?

It is clear that spirits hold a central place in shamanic practices, but we have not yet fully answered the question, 'What are spirits?' Several volumes could be written on this subject alone, and understanding the nature of spirits is by no means an easy task. Throughout history it has proven to be a profound theological and psychological challenge.

Spirit in the traditional shamanic sense usually has a dual meaning. When shamans refer to spirits, they usually mean the essence of something, the life force of something which speaks to them and helps them. However, spirit can also be perceived as consciousness: animals, trees, rocks and even seemingly inanimate objects can possess a consciousness which is similar to our own. Most cultures hold the belief that the soul of a living human becomes a spirit when the person dies. Upon death, the soul may either become an ancestor spirit or a part of a larger elemental spirit.

The actual word 'spirit' is derived from the Latin word *spiritus*, which literally means 'breath'. The Oxford dictionary defines 'spirit' as 'a supernatural, incorporeal, rational being or personality, usually regarded as imperceptible at ordinary times to the human senses, but capable of becoming visible at will, and frequently conceived as troublesome, terrifying, or hostile to mankind'. This definition reflects, to a large degree, many westerners' views on spirits. When asked about their understanding of spirits, many people on my workshops express either present or past fears of spirits. One person viewed spirits as bodiless souls of dead people. She was initially scared of these spirits because she believed the souls of those dead people to be lost.

Over the years, most people with whom I have talked about spirits reported similar beliefs. Spirits are usually perceived as ghosts and associated with fear. Some people would even go as far as viewing spirits as lost souls of dead people who have died in some tragic manner and return to this reality to claim justice or revenge. One person told me:

> As a child and an adult, spirits, ghosts and demons were synonymous to fear for me. Fear of the unknown and unfamiliar. When I think of spirits or ghosts I immediately think of the children's stories of my childhood, and about fears of what happens after death. Throughout my life I pre-

ferred not to think about these things. My rational and practical mind usually preferred to ignore things that were not explainable scientifically or rationally.

It seems that westerners tend to either not believe in the existence of spirits, or when they do believe in them, they generally think about ghosts and scary spirits and are afraid to meet them. This could be because of our cultural worldviews. I believe that people's interpretations and understanding of what spirits are rely largely on their cultural backgrounds. As we see from the dictionary definition, spirits in our culture are often perceived as malevolent to some degree.

Another way of understanding how we perceive spirits is by exploring the images of spirits appearing in the media. Spirits of many forms and kinds make frequent appearances on television or movie screens as well as in many books, stories and legends of our childhood. The most common form that appears in films and literary works is that of a spirit as a ghost of a dead person. *The Sixth Sense, Ghost, Casper, Hamlet,* and many others are examples. More rarely we also come across spirits of other forms, such as in the film *Harvey* and in the legend of King Arthur, where we meet the Lady of the Lake.

Many people ask me on workshops whether there are 'bad spirits' or if they are facing any danger by journeying shamanically. Throughout the years, I have never encountered a bad spirit during any of my journeys, and neither has anyone I have ever worked with. An Eskimo shaman once said that Sila, 'the soul of the universe [has] a voice so fine and gentle that even children cannot become afraid'.[1] When I am asked whether bad spirits exist or not I usually direct people to journey and ask their spirits teachers for an answer. When I myself asked my spirit teachers about the existence of bad spirits, I received an illuminating response:

'We are teachers and healers. Our job is to help. It's your interpretation. Sometimes people touch fear that we evoke in them, to help them become aware. If they cannot take that, they feel we are bad. It's people's interpretation. We are merely here to help and advise. Arvick, never give power to anything by calling it evil.'

One woman journeyed to ask what spirits are. Her teacher was Abraham. In the journey, she received the following teaching:

'Look at the stars. Just like the stars of heavens, the spirits twinkle, like sparks of knowledge, sparks of life.'

'Can these sparks hurt me? Are there harming spirits?'

'Feel the support of the earth, feel the support of the skies, that which supports you cannot harm.'

'I feel fear. What is that?'

'That is your imagination. That is your mind. People are the ones who make the choices. The fear is in you. We only hold goodness. Really, it is neither good nor bad. We hold sparks of knowledge and if you listen to this knowledge, you could make it your own.'

ARE SPIRITS REAL?

Finally, we reach the six-million dollar question: are spirits real entities existing separately from our own consciousness? Or are they simply a construct of our minds?

From a shamanic point of view, the answer to this question is a simple one. Spirits are living entities, external to us and separated from us, existing in an alternative reality to that which we usually experience. When journeying to the spirit worlds, shamans perceive and experience spirits to be separate entities, external to their own personal ego, with which they communicate and from whom they receive help. The shaman perceives the spirits as sources of information and healing which they cannot access by themselves.

I experience this most profoundly when I go on diagnostic journeys. At times, I perform diagnostic journeys for people who I have never met before, and of whom I have no prior knowledge. I also insist on not receiving any information about them before journeying. The messages I receive are always accurate beyond belief. We shall look more closely at diagnostic journeys in Chapter 5. Experiencing spirits as external entities is not unique to me, however. Many times on workshops, people come back feeling surprised about the message they have received from their teachers.

At times, before going on the journey, some people believe that they know the answers they will receive. When they receive answers that are not only different, but sometimes completely opposing their own assumptions, they are speechless.

For the westerner, the answer to the question 'Are spirits external to us?' is not as straightforward as it is for the shaman. People frequently doubt whether they are journeying and encountering 'real' spirits and believe that they are visualising and communicating with a part of their own psyche. Many times people return from journeys and even though they feel they have received significant answers, still question their experience and ask me: 'How do I know I spoke to spirits? Maybe it's just my imagination?'

As westerners, most of us were raised to believe that there is no such thing as spirits, in the sense that shamans perceive them to exist. Our education excludes any existence of invisible beings or entities, or in fact the existence of any invisible reality whatsoever. We are taught that reality is only what we perceive with our five senses while we are awake. As one person once shared with me:

> *As a little child I thought that spirits are little dwarfs that sit inside the radio and make it work or the little creatures that make the hands of the clock move. Then I learned that there is such a thing called God, and I thought he is this giant man that sits in the sky and never falls down. And I thought that he has those little creatures as his messengers, and they come to earth and hide in trees and flowers and under the ground. I thought that they were watching me and are able to see everything I do, and then they would go back to God and report to him. When I grew up I was made to understand that only what we perceive with our five senses is real, and that other realities and spirits, including those in movies and fairy tales are all nonsense.*

It is easy to understand why many people have problems believing the 'reality' of their own shamanic journeys. Even if one chooses consciously to believe in the existence of spirits, early education embedded deep within our minds almost inevitably affects our experiences and worldviews.

What is the alternative western understanding of spirits, then? We can find some answers in the explanations provided by health care professionals and social scientists. Traditional psychiatric or psychological approaches tend to interpret alleged encounters with spirit beings to be either hallucinations or manifestations of sub-personalities. Some therapists and psychologists actually use therapeutic methods which involve shamanic journeys, and yet do not believe that spirits exist as external entities to our ego. They tend to interpret shamanic journeys as a meeting with different aspects or parts of the person's personality and psyche, rather than with spirit entities.

Transpersonal psychologists tend to hold a slightly different view. Unlike the traditional psychologist, transpersonal psychologists might interpret a contact with what the shaman would call spirit helpers as coming into contact with transcendent aspects of our psyche, which lie 'above and beyond' our ego. They recognise the existence of the soul and respect its importance as a guiding force. This is what many people would call the 'higher self'; what Jung[2] would call the Self and what Gurdjieff[3] named the Essence.

But even transpersonal psychologists are not necessarily saying what the shaman claims – that the spirits are external entities we come into contact with. The higher wisdom that they admit we come in contact with could be perceived as separate from our ego and personality, but still not external to us. However, transpersonal psychologists do admit that it is possible to access wisdom from sources which surpass the ego and personality, and go to considerable lengths to connect with these sources.

Another popular approach westerners have adopted to explain shamanism and the spirits is by referring to Carl Jung's[4] work on the collective unconscious* and the archetypes.† However, I believe that a more broad analysis or understanding of Jung's writings could lead us to realise that Jung's concepts bear strong resemblance to those of shamans.

For Jung, the collective unconscious is a vast realm, parallel to Castaneda's[5] non-ordinary reality and the shaman's spirit world, encompassing much more than our own personal unconscious. It includes everything in existence. Jung also clarified that when spirits appear, whether they are a manifestation of the Self Archetype (a concept parallel to the soul) or are external entities, they nevertheless are *experienced* by the individual as external.

Jung also claimed that everything we experience is mediated by our psyche (composed of both personal and collective unconscious). It is obvious, then, that the spirits would appear to us as manifestations of the archetypes. However, that does not make them any less real! We can see, then,

---

* Jung distinguishes between the collective unconscious and the personal. While the personal unconscious is particular to each person, the collective unconscious refers to that part of a person's unconscious which is common to all human beings. It contains archetypes, which are forms or symbols that are manifested by all people in all cultures. The collective unconscious can be adequately explained as arising in each individual from shared instinct, common experience and shared culture. The natural process of generalisation in the human mind combines these common traits and experiences into a mostly identical substratum of the unconscious. For example, the archetype of the great mother would be expected to be very nearly the same in all people, since all infants share inherent expectations of having an attentive caretaker (human instinct); every surviving infant must either have had a mother, or a surrogate (common experience); and nearly every child is indoctrinated with society's idea of what a mother should be (shared culture). The amalgam of all these effects could be the source of the shared figure, or archetype.

† A Jungian archetype is a thought pattern that finds worldwide parallels, either in cultures (e.g. the similarity of the ritual of Holy Communion in Europe with the tecqualo in ancient Mexico) or in individuals (e.g. a child's concept of a parent as both heroic and tyrannical, superman and ogre). Jung believed that such archetypal images and ideas reside in the unconscious level of the mind of every human being and are inherited from the ancestors of the race. They form the substance of the collective unconscious, and are the images, patterns and symbols that rise out of the collective unconscious to appear in our dreams and fairy tales. There are four famous forms of archetype identified by Jung: the self, the shadow, the anima and the animus.

that Jung's perception of the universe and human consciousness is very similar to that of the shaman. In both cases, there is a normally hidden reality, which is the 'true' reality, lying beyond the ego. It is when we access this hidden reality that we are able to acquire wisdom which lies beyond the boundaries of our ego.

Having said all that, at the end of the day, could we really fathom the true nature of spirits? Can we answer the question: do spirits really exist as external entities? Are spirits the constructs of our mind or higher self, or do they exist outside our ego boundaries? No, we cannot. It is impossible, with the tools we have today, to either prove or disprove the existence of spirits in the shamanic sense. Basically, it is left to the individual and the individual's worldviews, beliefs and experiences to determine what it is exactly that they are encountering.

At this point I would like to quote Roger Walsh[6] who eloquently summarises the issue: 'In light of all this, the fact that we cannot decide once and for all about the existence of spirits, channels, and nonphysical entities is not so surprising. It simply reflects our current ignorance and perhaps even perpetual limitations on our knowing. This may not be terribly satisfying but it may be usefully humbling.'

I went on a journey to ask my spirit teachers to give me knowledge about the nature of spirits. The answer I received, however, reminded me again that the significance of spirits is not so much in what they are, as more as about what they do:

> *You cannot really define spirits. It is difficult to be scientific about spirits. You can explain in what form we appear, and what we do, how our help changes people's lives, opens windows in people's lives, opens their inner eyes, their inner*

ears, so they can see deeper into themselves and hear deeper, hear deeper messages. We help people to go into the realms of their mind, where they normally are not able to enter. You are all walking around with closed minds, with limitations that you have put on yourselves. So you are blinkered, you only see as much as you allow yourself to see. Because of the rules, of what is possible and what is not possible, that you are taught from a very young age. There are limitations about your capabilities. We give you and create the impossible; we help you to expand your mind, to see with no blinkers. The vista is expanded. You can see far, all around, not just in front. Your senses become sharper. By letting go and trusting, you enter the world that is not normally possible to enter. Imagine your head like a box – and we help the wall of the box disappear. So you see and reach with your eyes and ears beyond the box. Your mind expands.

IS SHAMANISM A SPIRITUAL PRACTICE?

Shamanism is humanity's oldest spiritual practice. But what does that really mean? What is a 'spiritual practice'? What is spirituality? And how can shamanic practices potentially lead us on our spiritual path? These are some of the questions we will be exploring in this section.

Many associate spirituality with religion. However, I believe that spirituality has nothing to do with any particular religion or religious dogma. To be spiritual does not require us to have a special place of worship, specific rituals and practices or a mediator between us and the divine. Every one of us can lead a spiritual way of life, regardless of any religion we may or may not be practising.

It is difficult to ascribe one all-encompassing definition of spirituality. Spirituality is essentially a private and personal matter. Each one of us has our own understanding and answer as to what spirituality means to us, and even that may change with time. Thus, I will not try to provide one single definition of spirituality. Instead, I will be presenting here the different teachings given by the spirits on the subject, and conclude with my current understanding on this matter.

Spirituality has always been one of the focal points in my shamanic workshops. Over the years, some students journeyed to the spirits, asking for teachings about spirituality. The messages people received were breathtaking, and I wish it was possible to present them all in this book. Regretfully, I am able to present here only a fraction of these beautiful messages.

The teaching on spirituality I present here was given to a woman by one of her spirit teachers. On her journey Nurit met various teachers – a carpenter working on a piece of wood, a mother feeding her baby, a stone in a river and King Solomon. They all had messages to share about what spirituality meant to them.

From the carpenter she received this message:

> *'Spirituality is what I am doing now, I am one with this wood, one with the movement of cutting this wood, one with my tools, totally present. I have put my stamp here and this piece of wood*

is my witness that I have taken part in the story of creation. That is spirituality for me.'

The mother feeding the child told her:

Spirituality for me is this baby that I brought to the world and am taking care of. I am responsible for his growth and to provide him what he needs for his own growth. It will be a part of an endless chain of generations that is taking part in the story of creation.

The stone said to her:

I am here, present. The water flows over me, sometimes strongly and sometimes very gently. I am transforming with the water and the winds but ever here. That is spirituality.

And finally, King Solomon himself spoke:

You have been to a few places; you have touched a very little part of my kingdom. I am the king – the conductor of this choir whose purpose is to witness the story of creation. I give my people the opportunities to take part in this creation and each one of them has their own share in this story. Every soul has its own role: to serve the eternal, to be a servant of holiness; that is spirituality, this is freedom. I am a king and my role now is to help people to master their own kingdoms. That is my mission. I am teaching them with poetry, with metaphors and through action; that is my role, this is spirituality for me. There is no difference. The spirit, the spiritual is the same, the stone, the water, the wood, the tools

– they are all the same, only the form that they take may change. To put it in your daily words, there are endless possibilities and choices in the universe and spirituality means to be able to be aware of them by mastering the physical, the emotional and the mental, and to choose.

It is clear that on this journey the spirit teachers provide Nurit with different ways of understanding spirituality. The following is what she understood from each of the metaphors and messages given to her. Nurit understood the message of the carpenter to indicate that:

Spirituality is when we are one, totally present, in harmony with the movement of the universe. By being in that state we are creating all the time. There is no judgement about what we create; each soul has its own role in that creation and every role is important as it contributes energy back to the universe.

Her understanding of the mother's words was:

Spirituality is like giving birth to things. Whatever we create, we are responsible to give it the maximum conditions for it to grow and by that we are contributing or taking part in the story of creation.

The message from the stone meant to her:

Spirituality connects us with our strength and power. In times of storms or calmness we are able to transform and change with nature, accepting the process of life and death as part of the endless change and movement of the universe.

And finally, her understanding of King Solomon's words was:

> *Spirituality integrates our different aspects. It is like being a conductor of the choir of life that has different sounds and voices. It means to master all our parts, all our emotions, and integrate them into our different worlds and by that make them holy – fulfilled and free. The meaning of spirituality is that the contents of our spirit are the same, only the forms that people bring into spirituality changes.*

As we can see from this journey, there are many different perspectives from which we can look at spirituality. When journeying to receive a teaching about spirituality, another person was given different messages on the subject.

Inbal was shown many islands floating around with a person standing on each of the islands. Each person on each island seemed oblivious to the existence of others around them. The teacher (in this journey, her guardian spirit) suggested:

> *You perceive that you are alone when you are not. Spirituality is learning to recognise what is, instead of what we think there is. These people believe that there is nothing around them, and so they perceive nothing to be around them, although that is not the actual truth. Take this image with you. It means, quite literally, that every single thing is not only alive around you, but is directly and powerfully connected to you, and influences you. Spirituality is the striving to recognise the truth, the true nature of things.*

Next, Inbal, accompanied by her guardian spirit, walks off the island and onto a path, leading to a large mansion. Along the way, a bandit, holding a large stick, jumps in front of them, and stands in the middle of the path, appearing menacing. He then asks:

'Where are you going?'

Her guardian spirit proceeded to explain:

Spirituality is also the conquest of fear. Why have you stopped midway, when there is plenty of way to pass? He is just standing here. This is ignorance. Spirituality is the conquest of fear and ignorance. It's a combination. The fear is standing here to stop you and your ignorance and lack of imagination is stopping you from walking right through it.

Ram Dass once described spirituality as 'a journey that is a progression from truth to ever deepening truth'. For me, this journey begins by discovering my own truth, having the courage to look into myself, to be honest with myself and others. Most of us find this very hard to do. It is not easy to be constantly honest with others, not to mention ourselves. But why is that? What is it that stops me from being honest with myself and others? What is it that stops me from looking in the mirror?

The two seemingly separate messages in the second journey address spirituality in relation to truth and to fear. These two themes, however, are very much linked, as a more in-depth exploration of the messages would demonstrate. Let us begin by exploring the role fear plays in our lives and how it might affect our spiritual growth.

The first fear we ever experience is the realisation, as young children, that the world is external to us, that we are separated from all that surrounds us. We realise that our mother is not us, that our food is not us, that everything and everyone that surrounds us, in fact, is a separate entity in their own right, existing outside of our control. The first experience of this separateness and fear could be traced back to our actual birth, when for the first time we were separated from our mother – the source of life and comfort.

However, this fear we feel on an existential level, the aloneness of being separated from all creation, is actually groundless. The fact is that we are all connected to each other and to everything, we are a part of all we see around us. This interconnectedness is actually acknowledged today by quantum physicists, and is explained in the journey presented above. We are simply blind to that fact, ignorant to our real state of existence

Fears manifest themselves and influence almost every aspect of our lives. Generally speaking, there are two umbrellas of emotions that we live under: love and fear. Most of us live under the umbrella of fear for most of the time. It is this fear that creates jealousy, anger, judgement, hate, guilt and all the emotions that we perceive and judge as bad or negative. Driven by fear, we become blinkered, narrow-sighted and disconnected from our own creativity and power. Fear prevents us from being honest with ourselves and others and from letting go of placating behaviours. Occasionally we manage to step under the umbrella of love and touch the true soul that is within us. It is then that we are in our true power, experience true generosity, compassion, understanding and all the other emotions that we judge and perceive as good or positive.

But what are we really afraid of? There is a multitude of things we *may* be afraid of. Fear of discovering things we may not like about ourselves, fear we may lose someone or something, that we may appear foolish, that we may not be accepted or liked, fear of failing, being humiliated or abandoned, fear of the unknown. Or as Susan Jeffers eloquently concludes in her book, *Feel the Fear and Do it Anyway,* 'At the bottom of every one of our fears is simply the fear that you can't handle whatever life may bring you'.[7]

Fear simply is a very 'scary' thing. We are afraid of fear itself and we are taught to avoid it at any cost. Yet in order to truly grow we must dare to confront our fears. On the journey, the only way for Inbal to continue walking on her path and reach her destination was to confront her fears, represented by the armed bandit. If we truly wish to live spiritually, we will have to eventually face our fears, and go through them. If we 'feel the fear and do it anyway', if we treat fear as a teacher rather than an enemy, we may learn the valuable lessons it has to teach us, and open our eyes to the truth about ourselves. It is only then that we will come to recognise our own power and beauty and take mastery over our lives.

And when we finally do that we discover that it is not fear itself that is stopping us, but ourselves. As the spirit teacher said, fear is simply standing in our path. But the truth is that there is nothing that is really stopping us from walking right past them. Fear is actually:

F = False

E = Evidence

A = Appearing

R = Real[8]

Our fears are our illusions, what we are so desperately afraid of is not real. When we face our fears, they inevitably lose their power over us and we discover that what we were afraid of is not really that scary. Fear is a barrier between us and the truth, between us and honesty, between us and self-fulfilment, because the picture we see of our world and of ourselves is distorted by it.

In this light, the islands metaphor given on Inbal's journey could be interpreted on a deeper level. If we look at it more closely we may realise that it is not only coming to teach us that we are all connected to each other, but also to propose that we simply do not perceive reality as it truly is. Or in other words, by using this metaphor the spirits may be telling us that we all live in an illusion. This is actually a very similar claim to that which many shamans make – namely, that the ordinary reality as we experience it is not the 'real' world, that it is a lie, an illusion, and that the real world lies in the non-ordinary realms of the spirits. It is in our ordinary reality that we are bound by the limitations of our ego, our belief system, comparisons and judgements, and ultimately, our fears. They are the tinted glasses we always wear, and through which we perceive and interpret our world. They are the tinted glasses which hide the true nature of our world from our consciousness.

Spirituality, the spirit teacher tells us, is striving to see the world as it truly is, free of these limitations. And it is when we confront our fears and go past them that we begin to gradually remove the layers of tint from our glasses.

It is clear, then, that we must acknowledge our fears in order to grow. But that is only one part of the story. It is also important for us not to *judge* our fears as wrong. Fear is a natural part of our lives, and to some extent it is necessary. Fear is actually a natural and healthy physiological response to danger. The problem begins when we perceive danger where it doesn't really exist. Hence our aim is not to totally rid ourselves of fears, but rather to have awareness of how they operate within us. The first step to freedom, then, is to recognise we have fears, and understand how they affect our lives. It is only then that we truly begin to tread on our own spiritual path.

Most of us have experienced moments in which we are totally present, free of fears. People refer to these experiences as 'spiritual experiences', but in fact they are moments in which we are simply experiencing ourselves and the world around us as we are and as it is, without comparison, judgement, resistance or fear. And the beauty of these moments is that they are nothing special. They can be very small, very simple, almost casual. I will never forget my first experience of the Grand Canyon. As I stood in the Arizona desert, looking at it, I was suddenly filled with a sense of awe and wonder. I was free of my mind and thinking. I felt a sense of smallness and humility and at the same time a very strong connection with everything around me. Never in my life had I felt so alive, so free and joyful.

Descriptions of experiences such as the one I had, and messages and teachings such as the ones the spirit teachers give us, can be found in any spiritual philosophy. Living according to these messages, or attaining a state of existence that is free from fear, however, is easier said than done. Being aware that we 'should' confront our fears doesn't necessarily help us do it. Awareness can be the first step in taking responsibility to bring these messages into our lives and, as the shaman says, 'to walk the talk'. But that is only the first step. Once we take this step, each one of us finds our own way or practice to help us continue on our spiritual path. For me that path is shamanism.

I would like to conclude this chapter with a message given to a woman on a journey by her guardian spirit:

> *This is what shamanism is about – bringing light and life into the dark places. Once you turn a small light on, it inevitably expands. The light brings warmth, the warmth brings life, life brings awareness, awareness brings connection, connection brings a truer vision of reality. A truer vision of reality brings peace of mind, and peace of mind brings love. And love is, of course, inevitably, spirituality.*

***

When I let go of fear,

I am light,

I am life,

I am vibrant and alive

I am vulnerable

I am powerful

I am grateful to be alive.

Winter 2001

5 *The Ancient and the Modern: Shamanic Healing*

The tragedy of man is what dies inside himself while he still lives.
Albert Schweitzer

In 1987 I moved from England to New York. The only and very first person who offered me a hand in friendship, was Sara, and we became good friends. She was engaged to a musician, and they were to be married shortly. One day she confided in me that Greg was suffering from acute back pains and asked me if I would be able to help him with hypnosis, as he had tried everything and no medical or complementary doctor had been able to diagnose the cause of the problem or treat it. I agreed and made an appointment.

The day before the actual meeting, at two o'clock in the morning, I received a distressed phone call from Sara. She informed me that they were in the hospital and that Greg had been diagnosed with cancer at a very advanced stage and was only given three weeks to live. As time passed, however, the three weeks extended to six, eight, and beyond. Greg was in a terrible state. He was attached to tubes and swollen to the point that you could not recognise him. Greg had a great deal to lose. His daughter was about to graduate, and his marriage was imminent. Understandably, he was unable to let go.

At the time, I was studying NLP (neuro-linguistic programming) and one of the students in my class had often talked about Reiki. I had no idea what he was talking about and had *no interest. One day, out of desperation, I approached John and asked him if Reiki could help Greg. He said he was not sure, but that he was willing to go and give him treatments in the hospital. On Thursday both Greg and Sara received a full Reiki treatment from John. On Friday night, for the first time in three months, Sara decided to go home and sleep, while Greg's sister remained at the hospital. While Sara was home, at midnight, Greg died peacefully.*

For me, this was the biggest healing anyone could receive. Following that experience I started getting interested in Reiki, learned it and became a Reiki master.

ILLNESS AND HEALING IN CROSS-CULTURAL PERSPECTIVE

Although the roles of the shaman are many and varied, the most important role they hold is, without doubt, that of a healer. The shamanic perception of health, illness and healing is a unique one. Although each culture practises its own specific forms of healing, certain communalities exist between all shamanic societies. In this chapter we will attempt to explore the basic understanding of both shamanic and western health care practices regarding illness, health and healing. We will also explore the different shamanic techniques used for healing and how they can be used to heal ourselves and others.

What is healing?

The definitions of the word 'healing' found in the Webster and Oxford dictionaries are: 'to make or become healthy, sound, or whole' and 'to restore to health; cure; become sound'. These definitions apply to the intention or function of virtually every therapy and medicine practised in the West today. However, the dictionary definitions, in this case, are too general to accurately convey the association most westerners may hold in regard to the word 'healing'. The fact is that the actual words 'healing' or 'healer' have no legitimate place in modern western medicine. The word 'healer' is often used in a derogatory manner and is usually associated with charlatans or quacks. When thinking of a healer the image that is more likely to appear in our minds is not that of a medical doctor, but rather of a tribal medicine man, or alternatively a practitioner of some complementary therapy.

Regardless of the connotations the word healing may have for westerners, however, the action of healing itself is hard to define, especially when we attempt to look at it from a cross-cultural perspective. That is because our definition of healing would inevitably depend on our cultural worldviews in general, as well as on our cultural definition of illness, disease and health, specifically. Thus, our preferred method of healing and the parameters of measuring the success of the healing procedure depend to a large degree on the culture we come from.

The difficulty in defining healing is not only due to cultural differences. Even within the cosmopolitan western medical system, not one definition of healing exists. Doctors and patients, for example, hold two different points of view by which they evaluate healing. While the doctor tends to identify biological change as the deciding parameter, patients put the emphasis on their subjective well-being, measuring the success of the healing procedure according to whether or not they 'feel better'.[1]

Life and death in shamanic healing

We have established by now that the shamanic worldview is considerably different in many ways from that of the modern western one. It is not surprising, then, that the shamanic concepts of health and illness differ considerably from those of modern health care practices.

The biggest difference between shamanic and modern societies is related to death and life in relation to healing. In shamanic cultures, healing is not necessarily the preservation of the physical body. The shaman is not concerned with the extension of life per se, but rather with achieving harmony between the ill person and all aspects of the cosmos. Achieving this harmonious and whole state may result in a physical recuperation and well-being, or may end with the person's physical death. For westerners, this view of healing is difficult to accept. The western view necessitates the preservation of life. Thus, a healing procedure which ends in death is considered a failed procedure. In fact, much of the western mistrust of shamanic healing is often the result of shamans' 'failure' to preserve their patient's life.

For the shaman, 'the course of life or death is irrelevant, for these are only different experiences along the one continuum of existence'.[2] From a shamanic point of view, then, even death can be healing. In fact, as we discussed in Chapter 2, at times, in order to achieve true healing, some kind of death must always be involved in the process of recovery, bringing about a transformation in the person.

Soul loss and spirit intrusion

Compared with modern medicine, shamanic healing traditions place a much greater emphasis on 'spiritual' disturbances. Healing, health and disease are all a matter of spirit. When attempting to heal, the shaman addresses the spirit realms in search of a cure and, since all health problems are related and connected to the state of one's soul, the majority of shamanic healing practices are focused primarily on the preservation, protection and nurturing of the soul. The two most common causes for disease and illness in shamanic cultures are either soul loss or spirit intrusion.

Soul loss, which is also called the 'rape of the soul' in certain cultures, may occur by the soul either leaving the body or having been stolen, captured or frightened away. Soul loss and soul retrieval will be fully discussed later on in this chapter. Spirit intrusions are instances in which either a magical object (such as an invisible dart) or a malevolent spirit have intruded into the body. Quite often, disease is perceived to occur as a result of initial soul loss which weakens the person in the first place, enabling a spirit intrusion to take place, further aggravating the person's condition. In both cases it is only the shaman who is able to offer help and cure, either by retrieving the lost soul or expelling the intruding bodies.

The belief in foreign spirits entering the body and causing disease is extremely common and can be found in different variations in many different cultures. The Evén of north eastern Siberia believe that illness is a direct result of the entrance of evil spirits into the human body. Such diseases as smallpox were believed to have a spirit in the form of a red-headed European-looking woman. Among the Wayapi, on the other hand, death was always blamed on a paje (shaman). The Wayapi believed that when upset with someone, the shaman would send his invisible darts to penetrate the person's body, causing their death.

The indigenous Anglo-Saxons also regarded disease as caused by spirit intrusion. This belief is evident in the concept of 'elf shot'; the Anglo-Saxons believed that a person may become ill as a result of being shot by elf arrows. Both the arrows and the elves were invisible to the layman's eye and only visible to the trained eyes of the shaman.[3] To heal a spirit intrusion the shaman would employ such means as sucking the offending element out of the body or journeying to the spirit worlds to fight against the invading spirit in an attempt to force it out of the body. The Yakut shaman, for example, attempts to scare and frighten the spirit out of the sick person's body, using loud noises and terrifying gestures.[4]

One of the fascinating techniques used by the Evén shamans involves transferring the spirit of the illness from the ill person's body and into a pair of wooden birds. During this procedure the shaman ensures that the birds journey to the upper world, taking with them the illness of the patient. The Evén believe that since the spirit of the disease is separated into two parts, it is prevented from ever returning into the person's body.[5]

This shamanic notion of health and illness is very foreign to the western mind. Most of us were raised to believe that the material world is the only existing reality. Any belief in spirits is considered to be a reflection of ignorance, primitive superstition, magical thinking or some form of regression to infantile functioning. Problems which are perceived by the shaman to originate in some sort of affliction in the person's soul and a diminishing of their power, would be explained by the western scientist as originating from psychological or physiological sources.

Disease and illness in shamanic perspective

Another difference between shamanic and western worldviews regarding health is related to the concept of disease. Disease, in the modern sense, is perceived as invading the physical body from the outside, and is regarded as something that must be eliminated, removed or destroyed. For the shaman, however, although an intrusion might be regarded as the cause of disease (such as an invisible arrow or bad spirit), the primary element which comes into consideration is the loss of personal power (or loss of soul) which weakens the person and allows the intrusion in the first place. All shamanic healings focus first on empowering and strengthening the sick person before removing or eliminating the harmful agent from their body or soul.

This view of illness is actually surprisingly similar to current and relatively recent notions in western medicine. While this wisdom has been available to shamans for centuries, it is only in the last few decades that western medicine has come to recognise that in order for different pathogens – such as viruses and bacteria – to be able to cause disease, the person's immune system must first be weakened enough to allow for actual illness to develop.

The most meaningful difference, however, between western medicine and shamanic medicine lies in the fact that shamans, unlike medical doctors, don't treat diseases. Shamans treat the whole person. Unlike the medical doctor who focuses on the physical aspects of the disease only, the shaman employs a more holistic approach to illness and healing. I often use a metaphor to explain the shaman's attitude towards human health, likening the human body to a chariot drawn by three horses, symbolising our emotional, mental and spiritual aspects. If the horses each pull in different directions an imbalance will be created which disrupts the functioning of the chariot, eventually leading to a total breakdown. If the three horses are running in unison, the chariot will remain balanced and continue its journey in harmony.

Thus, in attempting to identify the cause of the person's illness, the shaman closely examines the different aspects of the person's life, including the circumstances surrounding their life prior to the illness. The shaman would also show an interest in the patient's family and social circumstances, emotional states, any possible breaches of taboo, as well as any significant dreams they may have had. The medical doctor, on the other hand, focuses on discovering and verifying physical and chemical information about their patients, regardless of their psychological, spiritual and social situation.[6]

Arthur Kleinman,[7] one of the most prominent researchers in the field of health and illness, provides two separate definitions of illness and disease: he defines disease to be 'any primary malfunctioning in biological and psychological processes' while illness is 'the secondary psychosocial and cultural responses to disease, e.g., how the patient, his family, and social network react to his disease'.

From the very beginning of their training, medical doctors are taught to look at the symptom, the disease, the presenting condition rather than the effect the disease is having on the person's life. The shaman, however, treats not only the psychological or physiological manifestations of the disease itself, but is mindful also of the illness, and the effects the disease has on the ill person's life. Or, as a Mohawk elder once put it: 'The difference that exists is that the white doctor's medicines tend to be very mechanical. The person is repaired but he is not better than he was before. It is possible in the Indian way to be a better person after going through a sickness followed by the proper medicine'.[8]

The role of the community in shamanic healing

Another difference between shamanic healing and modern western health care practices is the role the community plays in the healing of the ill person. While in all fields of western health care patients are usually treated in total privacy, shamans prefer to treat their clients in the presence of their family or community. At times, the whole tribe participates in the healing ceremony of an ill person while, in some cases, family members may even take an active role in the healing ritual itself.

Regardless of culture, it seems that the support and love an ill person receives from others significantly aids their recuperation and healing process. The presence of the community in the healing ceremony, the concern and love of the tribe, facilitate the effectiveness of the healing ritual itself. It also serves to share the state of the ill person with the entire tribe and provide an opportunity for the afflicted person to receive love and support from their family and community even after the healing ritual is over.

Shamanic healing and psychosomatic illness

Most researchers would claim that shamanic healing only cures psychological problems, or at most, physical problems which have a psychological root – better known as psychosomatic problems (such as asthma, migraines, hives, rheumatoid arthritis etc.). Two points need to be addressed in relation to this. Firstly, shamanic healing is not limited to psychological or psychosomatic illnesses only. Shamans are known to heal also what we would consider to be severe physical diseases, such as diabetes and cancer. Secondly, a review of the term 'psychosomatic' is needed, since the distinction between 'real' physical problems and 'psychosomatic' ones is somewhat problematic.

The term psychosomatic has been and still is misused or misunderstood by many. When referring to an illness as psychosomatic we are simply suggesting that both the psyche (mind) and the soma (body) are involved in the creation of the disease. This relationship between psychological and physiological factors is not a causal one, but rather implies an interaction between the two factors. However, the term has commonly come to be used as indicating a physiological problem which is caused by a psychological one.[9] This is the basis for the common saying, 'Oh, it's all in your head.'

This is problematic for two reasons. One, because understanding psychosomatic to mean 'all in the head' or less than *real*, may result in a devaluation of the person's experience. This can give less credence to the reality of the person's sickness, often resulting in the person experiencing feelings of guilt because they may feel that they have wasted the doctor's precious time. People may also feel guilty for taking time off work, for example, when the doctor has not given a medical diagnosis for the illness. Second, there cannot be real distinction between diseases that are psychosomatic and diseases that are not. In fact, Pelletier[10] claims that up to 90 per cent of all disease has some psychological components.

Jeanne Achterberg,[11] one of the most interesting writers on the subject of shamanism and medicine, thus suggests that either the term psychosomatic should be defined correctly in the medical and psychological literature, or a new term should be introduced (such as 'psychophysiological') which clarifies the existence of interplay and interaction between the mental and the physical. She further claims that data collected from different fields such as physiology, biochemistry and quantum physics point to the fact that in fact no clear distinction can be made between mental and physical diseases: 'Mental/physical, body/mind, are false dichotomies, peculiar to our culture. Schizophrenics have biochemical abnormalities; does that make schizophrenia a physical or mental disorder? Cancer, diabetes, and heart disease have predictable psychological correlates. What category, then, must they be in?'

Common ground

At first glance there seems to be a great gulf between western and shamanic worldviews regarding illness and health. However, if we allow ourselves to look deeper into both practices, we may discover surprising similarities. Brian Bates, in his book *The Way of the Wyrd*,[12] draws attention to the similarities which exist between the two views. Both modern medicine and shamanic cultures view disease as a result of the weakening of the immune system/soul and the intrusion of invisible malevolent organisms/spirits into the person, causing the disease. In both cases the purpose of the healing is to extract or rid the person of the disease-causing agent. These disease-bearing agents (whether spirits or germs and viruses), reveal their pathogenic nature in presenting particular symptoms and can only be treated by being driven out of the body.

Bates goes on to compare the intrusion by malevolent spirits or invisible darts with the now widely accepted view of bacteria and viruses. Normally invisible, these harming agents can only be detected by a highly trained specialist, whose perception is enhanced by either technology, in the case of the physician, or an altered state of consciousness, in the case of the shaman.

HEALING IN THE EYES OF THE SPIRITS

I would like, at this point, to present some of the teachings of the spirits on the concept of healing. A dear friend of mine who was interested in the subject went on a journey to ask her spirits for teaching on healing. On this journey she found herself in the lower world and met a lizard, who was her teacher for the journey. Here are some of the main messages she received:

The lizard starts to run all over my body and tells me to lie down. She is going through my hair, walking on my eyes and putting her tongue into my nostrils and on my lips. Now she continues with the body, she is on my hands and belly, going down to the legs and licking each toe.

'Is there a message in this action?'

'I went over all of the places in your body in order for you to understand that every place is important, and healing is the ability to create equilibrium between all of them,' she answers.

The lizard starts running and asks me to run after her. She is running very fast and doesn't seem to be getting tired. I am running after her, running with big strides. She is moving lightly and with agility, not losing any energy. We are running in a desert and it is raining. Now the rain becomes strong, the sky is black. I feel tired. I am wondering when we will stop. Gradually, my strength is waning. Now I don't have any energy and I am standing; I allow myself to fall on the ground. I am totally wet and gradually a swamp is being formed around me. I feel that the ground beneath me is starting to get very muddy and I don't know what to do. I am afraid of sinking and afraid to continue by myself. I see her now coming closer, and she offers me a paw.

'Disease is loss of energy. It's like a black hole that sucks us like that mud was starting to suck you in. Your ability to keep energy inside yourself is what makes you healthy. The mud is related to the disease. The mud represents things that are mixed together in a wrong way.'

We start walking and reach a jungle. We are walking in the jungle and reach a place with many frogs. The frogs are green with red spots. They are jumping in the mud, and from the mud to the plants around them, and back.

The lizard tells me, 'These frogs have venom in the red spots. Just as the venom can kill, you could also create the antidote out of it. So the venom contains within it both aspects – that of the disease and that of the healing. That which exists in nature also exists in life, in the soul of human beings. All disease contains within it the essence which brings the healing. It is difficult for you to discover that. You are so afraid of the disease that you can't see the part of the disease that is meant to heal you. You are blind to it.'

We continue walking and reach a clearing in the forest. I see people fighting with snakes, with something that looks like a snake, but it's not really; it is some kind of a squirming monster. The lizard tells me to observe it. I am looking at them. At first it is a bit scary and not pleasant to see, but gradually this sight is becoming more and more pleasant and comfortable. I realise that they are not really fighting, but that they are merging and twining inside one another. The monster is crawling and squirming and the man is squirming with it, and at one point they are rolling on the ground. Now everybody is lying on the ground and stops moving.

'In the process of healing, instead of fighting, you need to accept. You think that to be healed is to fight the disease, but really, to be healed means to soak the disease into you in a way that would cause it to stop existing. Disease is a result of either excess or lack, and healing lies in the balancing of them; in the balancing of the excess and the lack. If you fight the disease and don't accept it, if you don't understand it and what it is trying to tell you, then you cannot be healed.'

The function of any society's health system is ultimately tied to the philosophical convictions that the members hold regarding the purpose of life itself. For the shamanic cultures, that purpose is spiritual development. Health is being in harmony with the world view. Health is an intuitive perception of the universe and all its inhabitants as being of one fabric. Health is maintaining communication with the animals and plants and minerals and stars. It is knowing death and life and seeing no difference. It is blending and melding, seeking solitude and seeking companionship to understand one's many selves. Unlike the more 'modern' notions, in shamanic society health is not the absence of feeling; no more so is it the absence of pain. Health is seeking out all of the experiences of creation and turning them over and over, feeling their texture and multiple meanings. Health is expanding beyond one's singular state of consciousness to experience the ripples and waves of the universe.[13]

HOW SHAMANS HEAL

Shamanic healing techniques have always been used alongside more 'mechanical' forms of healing and medicine. The shaman would usually be consulted only when more simple and common forms of treatment failed, or when the illness presented clearly belonged to the realms of shamanic expertise. From the very dawn of humanity, human beings knew how to use plants to alleviate a variety of sicknesses, how to perform crude surgery and remove offending bodies (such as tumours, bullets, arrows etc.). The shamans would traditionally be placed at the top of the medical hierarchy in shamanic societies, due to their healing techniques which involve contact with the spirit world. Healers whose skill rests solely on mechanical manipulations or administration of plant medicine usually were placed at the bottom.

As discussed earlier, the shaman believes that illness is the result of loss of power or some damage to the person's soul or spirit. The most common disorders with which shamans deal are soul loss, loss of power, and illness caused by a spirit or power intrusion of some sort. Although the basic form of shamanic healing is through the shamanic journey, there are a variety of different journeys and healings that the shaman employs when working with a person, depending on the presenting problem. We will now explore the variety of ways we can use shamanic techniques in order to heal different problems.

Two classic healing techniques used in shamanic practice are the soul retrieval and power animal retrieval. In both cases an essence is returned or introduced into the person, for the purpose of either enhancing power and abilities or completing the soul or spirit of the person. We will now explore in depth both techniques and the ways in which they are used to heal.

SOUL LOSS

For the shaman, most serious illnesses are the result of soul loss or power loss. Fear of losing soul or having it captured or stolen pervades most cultures that practise shamanism. The belief in soul loss is based on the idea that human beings either possess many souls or that the one soul may fragment and certain parts of it may leave the person. Shamans believe that loss of soul results in loss of power. The more souls that are lost, the more powerless and weak one becomes. In many cultures a severe soul loss is believed to result in death.

But what is a soul, really? Although we are all familiar with the term, as noted earlier in this chapter, the nature of the soul, or in fact its actual existence, is largely questioned in western cultures. Answering this question is of course a personal matter. For me, the soul is our essence, our very life force and the source of our vitality. It is my centre of being and thus my power.

Different cultures hold different views as to the nature of the soul. One such popular belief is that all living creatures possess *two* souls. One soul resides in our body permanently and takes care of the automatic primary bodily functions, such as breathing and homeostatic regulation of the different body systems. The second soul is the free soul which leaves our body to roam the spirit realms while we dream or while journeying shamanically.

However, it is important not to generalise. Different cultures may hold extremely different beliefs regarding the number or nature of our soul or souls. While some may believe that we possess only two soul parts, others believe that we have many. Among the shamanic peoples of North Asia, it is believed that a person may possess as many as three to seven separate souls. At death, while one soul remains in the grave, another descends to the lower worlds while a third ascends to the upper worlds.[14]

The Kalinia of the Orinoco area of Venezuela believe that the human soul (the *Askari*) has an animalistic aspect, also called the 'double' or 'friend'. At night, the animal double travels outside of the sleeping person's body and goes to visit its own animal family, telling the sleeping human soul of its nightly adventures. That way, the sleeping person learns and gets to know the souls of the animals. The *Askari* is just as vulnerable as the body is. The Kalinia believe that the great ancestral grandfather protects the *Askari*, but that under certain circumstances it is possible for it to get hurt or even abducted, never to return to its physical body. If the *Askari* leaves the body and does not return, the person gets sick and eventually dies.[15]

This is a classic example of soul loss and the dramatic effects which it may have on the person. To put it simply, when losing soul we in fact lose vitality and power. That is because when we lose a part of our essence we are no longer complete and whole. While we may at times lose soul and gain it back, other times it may not return on its own. It is in cases such as this, when permanent soul loss occurs, that shamanic intervention becomes necessary.

But how do we recognise soul loss? The effects of soul loss are not always immediately apparent. Some of the possible immediate symptoms are feelings of disconnectedness from our surrounding, from people around us, our closest family and, most severely, from ourselves. At times people who have suffered soul loss may appear to be living in a dream world or experience numbness and disconnection from emotions. The majority of indigenous cultures, including Siberian tribes, describe experiences of having the soul frightened out of them, as a feeling of being alienated from themselves and losing themselves. In psychological terms, states of dissociation or depression would be considered by shamans to be classic symptoms of soul loss.

However, soul loss may also have long-term effects. Memory loss, for example, could be a symptom of soul loss. In this case, severe soul losses which occurred in our past may have led us to forget either specific events or even a whole period of our lives. At times people I work with claim that they are unable to remember anything about their childhood. This is usually an indication that soul loss has occurred. Acute feelings of low self-esteem or powerlessness as well as destructive behavioural patterns such as various addictions, may also point to the possibility of soul loss. Massive soul loss may also cause people to repeatedly attract people into their lives who are in some form or another more powerful than they are. Having said all that, we are not robots; we are all different and react differently to experiences in our lives. Soul loss, then, would affect each of us in a different way. Thus, at the end of the day, the question of whether or not soul loss is the cause of any of our presenting symptoms is best answered by the spirits.

We may lose souls in a variety of ways. One of the main causes for soul loss is trauma. This may be a traumatic experience of any kind, and may occur at different ages and stages of our lives. We are all exposed to potentially traumatic experiences. We may lose souls as a result of shocks, bad news, a relationship break-up or the death of a loved one, accidents, major illnesses, birth traumas, domestic violence, physical, emotional or sexual abuse and other traumatic experiences. The trauma need not, however, be dramatic. One can lose one's soul for something as little as a sudden fall, a startling situation or a fearful walk in the dark.

Basically, it could be said that souls may depart as a result of either experiences of loss or experiences of fear in our lives, or any other experiences which bring about disharmony and loss of equilibrium.

Evidence for such experiences of soul loss is ample in our daily language. We often hear people say, 'When my husband left me a part of me went with him', or, 'When my brother died, a part of me died with him.' Following fearful experiences, people often say, 'God, I was scared to death when that happened.' Other expressions such as 'I just felt I wanted to die' or 'What she did really broke my spirit' may also be indications that a soul loss has occurred.

We may lose souls not only as a result of trauma, but because we may simply give them away. Whether as children or as adults, people frequently find themselves in situations where, in order to please others and be accepted, they compromise who they truly are or what they truly wish to do. However, by doing that they are very likely to lose parts of their soul. Other cases in which we may give soul away are situations in which we feel powerless. If we find ourselves in a relationship where we experience being less powerful in some aspect compared to another person, whether as children or adults, coming from a disempowered position, we may give parts of our soul away.

People of shamanic cultures believe that souls can also be hunted and captured. The Jivaro, for example, regularly indulge in the practice of soul capture in order to increase their personal power.[16] The Menangkabau tribe of Sumatra believe that illness may be caused by the theft of the soul by either gods, demons or particular spirits.[17]

Souls can be lost at different stages of life – starting with infancy and up until late adulthood. We may lose a soul even before we are born. One story which beautifully demonstrates this is that of Ray.

On a diagnostic journey I did for him, the spirits told me Ray had deep fears embedded in the cells of his body. They instructed me to perform a soul retrieval, to help him heal these fears. When I journeyed to retrieve the soul for him, I found, to my amazement, an 8-month-old foetus. This was the first time I had experienced retrieving a soul of a baby still in the uterus. When I returned from the journey Ray told his mother what had happened. She was amazed and explained that during the eighth month of her pregnancy with him, she was left by herself in a foreign country where she had no relations and family support, except for one friend. Her husband had to travel to another country and she was supposed to travel after him. She was very young, it was her first pregnancy, and she was absolutely terrified of giving birth without her husband or any close members of her family being present.

She experienced a fear so intense it was close to terror, and the worst thing was that she couldn't share this fear with anyone because she didn't want to alarm or upset her husband or family. Even now she remembered that time as one of the worst times in her life, and that experience as one of the most frightening ones.

As we have seen, we may lose souls for a variety of reasons, but the question still remains: why, when faced with disempowering situations, does our soul or part of it leave us? Sandra Ingerman,[18] in her comprehensive book about soul retrieval, *Soul Retrieval: Mending the Fragmented Self*, claims that soul loss is basically a matter of adapting or surviving. When confronted with an acutely disempowering situation, our natural response is to attempt to regain our power.

However, at times we are in such a weak state that we are unable to act accordingly. It is then that the soul part of us which is affected the most by the disempowering situation might leave us. For example, we may be working in a place under a boss who we may experience as too harsh or abusive. Our natural wish in a case like this would be either to confront our boss or to quit the job and rescue ourselves from the unpleasant situation. However, this may not be so easy. We may have fears of confronting our boss or a fear of not being able to find another job. Faced with a situation such as this, the soul part which is most affected by this reality may leave us. This is a survival mechanism because, by leaving, that part is assuring not only its own survival, but also the survival of our entire self and soul. This mechanism can actually be explained using two other popular psychological theories.

We can relate the concept of soul loss to Jung's concept of the shadow self. The Jungian shadow self is a term used to describe the accumulation of the rejected fragments of our psyche. Throughout our lives, Jung claimed, we lose parts of our own psyche, parts which for one reason or another we deny or refuse to acknowledge as our own. These parts are repressed and pushed into the depths of our unconscious mind. For example, if a little girl shows aptitude for engineering, but instead is encouraged to become a nurse, Jung would say that the part of her which wanted to become an engineer was repressed and has become a part of her shadow self. This could be likened to the shaman's concept of soul loss. Just like for Jung the part of the psyche is repressed to the subconscious, for the shaman the soul part flees the body and is lost. In order to complete ourselves, Jung claimed, a process of reintegration of these lost parts must take place. The integration of the shadow with the true self then results in psychological wholeness and well-being.[19]

Soul loss can also be likened to the psychological term of dissociation. Dissociation refers to a splitting of a part or parts of the psyche as a result of a traumatic experience. For the psychologist, dissociation would cause parts of the psyche (feelings, impulses or thoughts which are experienced as threatening), to be banished into the unconscious mind. For the shaman, the splitting which occurs is that of the soul, and the fragmented soul parts reside not in the psyche, but in an altogether different dimension of reality.

SOUL RETRIEVAL

In the case of soul loss, the shaman will embark on a journey to the spirit realms with the purpose of retrieving the lost soul or soul part, and returning it to the ill person. Different methods of retrieving lost souls are practised in different cultures around the world.

The Telut shaman attempts to restore the soul by calling it back to return to its body. While calling the soul of a sick child the shaman is crying, 'Come back to your country . . . to the yurt, by the bright fire! Come back to your father . . . to your mother!',[20] while in certain cultures it may be sufficient for the shaman to only call the soul, cajole or persuade it to return to its body. At times, and especially when the soul is reluctant or unable to return, the shaman may need to follow their initial call by actually journeying and descending into the underworld to bring the soul back.

In other cultures, the shaman will always journey to the spirit realms in search for the lost soul. The Tremyugan shaman begins his healing ceremony by the beating of his drum and playing the guitar. He then journeys to the underworld to search for the soul, where he will bargain with the souls of the dead for it. The shaman will either try to buy the soul by the giving of gifts or may attempt even more extreme means when forced to. Returning to the ordinary reality with the person's soul captured in his right hand, the shaman proceeds to blow it back into the person's body through the right ear.[21] The Lolo shaman in China, or the Karen shaman of Burma, on the other hand, read a long litany, imploring and begging the person's soul to return from its place of wandering.[22]

Just as losing a soul is one of the gravest injuries to a person, so is the work of soul retrieval one of the most important, challenging and responsible tasks for the shaman. Practitioners of core shamanism who wish to retrieve souls for others must first be properly trained and thoroughly understand the responsibility of the task facing them. During their initial training, shamanic counsellors acquire a special teacher for soul retrieval who always accompanies them and their guardian spirit during the soul retrieval journey.

In addition, certain rituals usually need to be observed prior to embarking on the actual journey. These differ from practitioner to practitioner. The particular instructions about the nature of the rituals are given to the counsellor by their own spirit teachers during their initial training and may also change with time. Basically, the purpose of the rituals is to focus the shamanic practitioner on the mission at hand and to prevent their energy from being dispersed. The full importance of pre-journey rituals was discussed at length in Chapter 3.

Unlike other types of journey, soul retrievals can only be carried out by a shaman or shamanic counsellor. Although spontaneous soul retrievals are known to have happened, it is generally not possible for us to purposefully journey and retrieve a soul for ourselves. This may seem like a form of dependency and appear to some as a contradiction to the basic claim that core shamanism is centred on self-empowerment. In our culture, independence or being self-sufficient are values that are held very dearly. Asking for help is perceived as being dependent and is judged by many to be a form of weakness. However, the fact is that we are not independent creatures. If it weren't for all the people and the elements which support us in our daily living, we would not be able to survive. We are all dependent on the very air we breathe, on the tap which directs water to our homes and the supermarkets which supply us with food. The fact is that as our world becomes increasingly modernised, so are we becoming increasingly dependent on others and other things around us. We are all connected to everything around us, but we have lost the humbleness of acknowledging that we are supported by the universe, and as a result, have lost the humbleness of asking for help.

Maintaining the wholeness of our soul is of supreme importance for our well-being and health. Any soul loss which occurs during our lives weakens us and exposes us to potential psychological or physical illnesses. Loss of soul can also affect our future life, even if the effects of the loss are not apparent immediately. When we lose a soul, at any time of our lives, a hole is created in our soul body. However, providing that the soul loss is not extremely massive, we manage to survive and lead a reasonably good life.

We may live with these holes or weaknesses for a while until something happens in our lives which requires us to draw on the missing energy in our soul body. These are usually challenging times in our lives which demand us to be strong and whole in order to be able to cope with the situation. If the particular energy we need to draw on is missing in our soul body as a result of earlier soul loss, we then react with either physical or psychological illness. This is because we lack the particular energy we require to cope with the situation at hand. Many times I have come across people who were experiencing hardships or going through a particular crisis, and when I went on a soul retrieval journey I had to retrieve a soul that was lost at a much earlier age.

Another way of looking at soul loss is by likening the soul body to a containing vessel. If we suffer multiple soul losses, our soul body is no longer an effective vessel, but rather functions more as a sieve. In this case we are not able to retain power within us; we gradually weaken and eventually develop a sickness.

Yarin, an 8-year-old boy from Israel, was referred to me for persistent and severe symptoms. For about eight months prior to our first meeting he had been defecating and urinat-

ing uncontrollably, and seeing insects in his food, which frequently stopped him from eating. Various psychological interventions failed from helping Yarin with his problem. I did a diagnostic journey which gave a very positive prognosis and in which I was instructed to perform a soul retrieval and power animal retrieval for the boy. I was also given instructions to do certain artwork with him.

Following the diagnostic journey and a piece of artwork, I performed a power animal retrieval followed by a soul retrieval. All in all, I met Yarin four times. At the time, the war in Iraq had just started and there was fear that the Iraqis would bomb Israel with chemical weapons. The country was in turmoil and everyone was instructed to carry gas masks and be prepared for a possible attack. From the artwork it became clear that Yarin was afraid of the possible harm to his parents and siblings in the case of an attack. The soul I brought back for him was that of a newly-born baby.

After I returned from the journey his mother told me that Yarin was born with two front teeth and that shortly after his birth the doctors extracted the teeth. Almost immediately after the soul retrieval, Yarin stopped seeing insects in his food. Gradually after that he also stopped defecating and urinating uncontrollably. What we can conclude from this is that shortly after he was born, Yarin suffered a significant soul loss. Obviously, as a baby he had suffered extreme fear as a result of the extraction, and then when the war brought up deep fear for him again, the relevant soul part or energy that he needed to draw on was missing. The soul having been returned to him, he was able to draw on that power and deal effectively with his present situation.

Carmen, a 40-year-old Spanish woman, was referred to me after having suffered a psychotic episode.

Carmen's breakdown had occurred following the death of her nephew. The healthy 20-year-old young man died suddenly of a heart attack with no previous medical history. The death was a great shock to his entire family, but Carmen was affected more severely than the others. Shortly after her nephew's death she was admitted to the hospital. After a few weeks she was discharged having been diagnosed to have suffered a psychotic episode and was prescribed psychotropic medication.

On my diagnostic journey, soul retrieval was recommended alongside other suggestions for treatment. I did a soul retrieval journey for Carmen two days after the initial diagnostic journey. The soul I found was that of a 3-year-old child. This made complete sense to Carmen. She told me that when she was 3 she developed double pneumonia and almost died. In fact, at one time during her illness she actually stopped breathing. Her mother shook her or did something and after a short while she started breathing again. She had a very important realisation regarding her experience. She said that she was aware that the death of her nephew triggered a deep fear of death that she had in her. The fact that the soul I had retrieved was that of a 3-year-old was particularly significant for her, because at that age she had actually experienced death.

Carmen was given specific rituals to do following her soul retrieval for one month. One month later she visited me again and told me that her medication had been reduced to a negligible dose and that she was feeling significantly better. Two months later, following the instructions in my diagnostic jour-

ney, I performed a power animal retrieval for her, to help her to connect with her inner power. A few weeks later she totally recovered and stopped taking her medication.

Finally, I would like to address a few important points regarding soul retrieval work. At times, people may read a book about shamanism and conclude that they are suffering from soul loss. They may come to a shamanic practitioner asking specifically for a soul retrieval. However, that is not the way to go about these matters. One of the major lessons that I have learned regarding shamanic work is that nothing is automatic. Even if I decide or assume that a person may need a soul retrieval, when I journey, my teachers may advise me differently. It is always for the spirits to decide whether and when one should undergo soul retrieval, and also whether any other shamanic work is needed to be done prior to the soul retrieval journey itself.

Another important point that I would like to stress here is that although soul retrieval is very powerful work and one of the most important shamanic healing interventions, it is not about quick fixes (as is the case, of course, with all shamanic work). We are not machines to be fixed. My experience to date has certainly taught me that as long as I am alive and breathing, life will have ups and downs. Soul retrieval will not result in us leading a quiet, sedate and uneventful life, devoid of all 'negative' emotions. What we may achieve through shamanic work is the ability to deal with situations more effectively, coming from our power and wisdom, rather than allowing situations in our lives to victimise us.

RITUALS TO EMBODY A SOUL

Soul retrieval is one of the most powerful shamanic interventions, because when receiving a soul back, we are regaining a great deal of our lost power. This is not a simple process. Integrating the lost soul back into ourselves may prove to be a challenging task. Just as the retrieved soul brings back the power which we lost, it also may bring with it the pain or the memory of the circumstances in which it was lost. Thus, to successfully integrate the soul back, we need to make it feel welcome. For this reason it is advisable for people who undergo soul retrieval to have a support system of some sort, whether family members, friends or a therapist, to help and support them through the process.

Another way in which we can facilitate the process of integration of the retrieved soul is by performing a ritual for some time following the soul retrieval. The instructions for the rituals are given to the shaman or shamanic counsellor during the soul retrieval journey and must be performed by the recipient of the soul. They are performed specifically in order to embody the soul and prevent it from being lost again, and vary from person to person.

Generally, in shamanic healing, it is important for the person seeking help not to be a passive recipient of healing but rather to participate actively in the process. Just as in western medicine one needs to take medications regularly in order to get well, so the person seeking shamanic help must perform the rituals assigned to them by the spirits in order to facilitate their own transformational process. Performing a ritual to facilitate the embodiment of the soul both commits the person to their own healing and allows them to become an active participant in the process.

At times, people become attached or used to their own misery or to a particular way of living. Although on one level they are not happy with their situation, and wish for a change in their lives, on another level they are not always so willing to let go of the state they are in. As the famous saying goes, 'Better the devil you know...' Hence, performing the ritual is a way of communicating to the soul part as well as to ourselves that we are willing to allow the transformation to take place in our lives. The ritual thus serves as a vehicle for transformation, allowing the person to move from the old to the new, marking the death of the old self and the birth of the new one.

In addition, in some cases I believe that the ritual itself is helping the person to heal the effects that the soul loss has had on their behaviour. For example, a woman I once worked with was requested to stand in front of a mirror twice a day, and pretend that she was talking to different people in her life, asking for very important things from them. She was instructed to imagine that the person she was pretending to talk to was at times giving her a positive answer and at times a negative one, and to observe her reactions to the imaginary answers each time. In the journey, the spirits explained that the soul loss she had experienced disempowered her in a fashion which affected the manner in which she communicated her discontentment with people. Thus the ritual itself not only supported the integration of the soul, but also helped her to wake up, observe her behaviour, and eventually let go of it. Rituals can serve as a powerful tool to help people release the patterns and behaviours which no longer serve them in their lives. Ritual, by nature, is a catalyst for change.

POWER ANIMALS

In the same way that we may lose souls, we are prone to lose power due to different experiences we may have throughout our lives. Losing power would inevitably expose us to illness, since our soul body is less than whole. The powers granted to the shaman by their power animals and guardian spirit are serving them as a form of protection against illness and disease. The reason, according to Harner,[23] is simple: 'it provides a power-full body that resists the intrusion of external forces. From the shamanic point of view, there is simply not room in a power-filled body for the easy entrance of the intrusive, harmful energies known in ordinary reality as diseases . . . Being power-full is like having a force field in and around you, for you are resistant to power intrusions, the shamanic equivalent of infections.'

When we are filled with power we are not only immune to diseases but are also in contact with our intuition and are not operating from our fears. Among the Jivaros, Harner elaborates; a power animal not only serves as a protection against disease, but also brings about an increase of alertness, self-confidence and honesty.

In the case of power loss, the shaman or shamanic counsellor will embark on a power animal retrieval journey and return the missing power to the person. Just as the medical doctor might prescribe vitamins to build up our immune system, so the shaman builds up the strength of their client by a retrieval of a power animal.

We may need a power animal retrieval either due to a loss of power, or in a case when we need to increase our power in certain areas. A power animal retrieval may aid us in a variety of ways. For example, if a person is experiencing problems concentrating, a power animal may be retrieved to enhance their ability to concentrate. At times, a power animal retrieval is necessary when a person needs extra power to deal with a certain situation in their lives. At other times, we may need a power animal retrieval before having a soul retrieval done for us, in order to prepare ourselves to receive and contain the soul.

What is power?

Health and illness are, for the shaman, a matter of power. While losing power brings about illness, gaining power enhances well-being. But what do we mean by 'power' in this context? Many people often question the concept of power, when first introduced to it in relation to shamanic work. For many of us, the word 'power' holds negative connotations. Often people associate it with violence, exploitation and coercion. Since the concept of power is very central in shamanic thinking, clarifying its nature is of the utmost importance.

It is true that power can be used for violent means. However, it has another aspect to it. According to Horwitz,[24] in Danish and German there are two separate words to denote the word 'power'. One is the word Macht which closely translates into the English word 'might'. The other is Kraft, which translates as 'energy' or 'creativity', and is similar to the English word 'craft'. Macht is the manipulative power people use in their attempt to control or influence others or their surroundings. Behaviours which stem from Macht power are behaviours which are stemming from fear. It is fear that is in the root of our manipulative power. Kraft, on the other hand, is a power which stems from love. It is the power of our creativity, which is not directed at anything outside us, but rather simply is. When we are power-filled, it is our creative Kraft power we are experiencing. In this state, Macht does not even exist.

Retrieving power animals

Unlike souls, which can be found either in the lower or upper world, power animals are to be found exclusively in the lower world. A power animal retrieval can be undertaken by the person who seeks the power themselves, and not only by the shaman or shamanic counsellor, as is the case with soul retrievals. There is virtually no limit to the number of power animals one can have. Throughout the years we may accumulate quite a crew of them. In indigenous cultures, the number of power animals shamans possess varies from culture to culture and from shaman to shaman, ranging from a few to dozens.

Invariably, when we journey for a power animal, we encounter energy in the form of an animal. However, at times, and mainly in diagnostic or healing journeys, the spirits have given me and others energy in the form of crystals, gemstones or flowers to bring back for a person. What is the significance of the particular form of energy we encounter and bring back, then? Are certain animals more powerful or helpful than others? I believe that although there is meaning and significance to the particular animal we retrieve, there are no weak or powerful animals. Each animal form has a service depending on the needs of the person.

Another important point to address is animal symbology. Some books about shamanism provide explanations of the meaning and significance of different animals. This, however, is misleading. Each culture has its own set of symbology regarding animals. Westerners often associate lions with bravery and majesty and a mouse with cowardice or shyness. This may not be true in another culture. In Iran, crows carry an altogether different meaning than they do for the Navaho Indians. A frog, a lizard or a snake are considered very powerful animals in certain South American tribes, but may mean absolutely nothing to a modern westerner. While journeying shamanically, it is wrong of us to assign set interpretations as to the meaning and symbology of animals. The best thing we can do is simply ask the animal directly while we journey – what is their role and how can they help us or the person we journey for?

Lastly, it is important to know that no power animal, no matter how fierce or powerful, would ever present any danger or cause any harm to the person who receives it. Power animals are simply that: a source of power. They come to us because we seek them and their intentions are always positive, and never malevolent. They are there to help us.

Why animals? Shamanism and the animal kingdom

What is the reason that we encounter power in the spirit realms in the form of animals, rather than in the form of humans? Why are our power animals, power animals?

It did not take Charles Darwin to persuade shamans that humans and animals are related. The connection between humans and animals is a given reality in shamanic cultures. People in such cultures not only live side by side with animals, but they also maintain a close and complex relationship with them. Many myths tell of a time when animals and humans conversed together, and many stories feature animal characters in human forms, living and interacting with humans. While this coexistence is no longer a reality in our daily life, it still is accessible to the shaman in the realms of the non-ordinary reality.

Through their guardian spirits or power animals, the shaman is able to form a connection with the animal power, which is otherwise not accessible to humans. Among the Kalinia tribe of Venezuela, it is believed that certain animals, or more accurately the spirits of certain animals, are extremely powerful. This power or wisdom emanates mainly from the animals' transformational capacities (such as snakes who shed their skin and are reborn, or frogs that can live both in water and on land), and is likened to the power of the shaman. It is said that the ancestors of the animals granted them powers which only the shaman had. Just like the animals, the shaman is capable of transformation and is able to transform into an animal or a bird.[25] Many cave paintings portray that relationship between the shaman and animals – paintings in which a half animal half human form is depicted.

Historically, human beings have always lived side by side with animals and were dependent on them for different aspects of their material existence. A close relationship has always existed between humans and animals and our ancestors relied on animals not only for food and clothing, but also for purposes of transportation, medicine, manufacturing of tools and plain companionship. Animals were also depended upon for purposes of 'weather predictions' and helped humans, through their behaviour, to foresee any forthcoming natural disasters.

Animals were not only needed; they were also feared and respected by early humans. Our ancestors observed that animals possess special abilities, strengths and powers, such as humans can never have. We could never swim as fish, climb rocks as deer, see as acutely as a hawk, run as fast as a cheetah, or soar into the skies like an eagle. We are of nature, just like our animal brothers and sisters, but we are also apart from it. Inhibitions, self-doubt, rationalisation, judgement and self-destruction are concepts unique to human beings. Animals are free of them, living their lives as they were meant to; they possess that raw natural energy which we humans have lost. Animals do not know the meaning of disconnecting with their spirit; they never lose the sense of themselves, and always maintain a connection to their surroundings and the nature around them, responding to all aspects of life. It is not surprising, then, that our ancestors considered animals to possess power, wisdom and a special connection to life, which we do not and cannot have, and thus turned to the spirits of those animals for guidance and teaching.

Although in this modern age we have grown apart from nature and animals, we still maintain a connection with them, through zoos, television or nature reserves, and of course pets. Children dream more often of animals than of humans, and show great affinity and liking towards them. Both live animals and puppet animals are used extensively in a variety of modern therapies with both children and adults. It appears, then, that the connection we historically shared with animals is still imprinted in the depths of our psyche, echoing to this day.

A story from Greece tells of the special relationship between humans, animals and the spirits.

Since human beings were mere mortals, the gods, looking down at them and seeing things that the humans could not see, would occasionally decide to send help and information to aid them in their lives. They did this through a woman called 'The Mother of Dreams'. The woman's task was to take the messages sent by the gods, wrap them each night within the skins of animals and send those animals into the dreams of the sleeping people for whom they were intended. If observant, the person who received such a message would remember the dream, remove the skin of the animal by interpreting the dream and listen to the gods' message. If the dream was not remembered, however, the animal would return to the Mother of Dreams. She would then attempt to send the animal back into another dream, until the message was heard. If even that did not avail, she would wrap the message in the skin of yet another animal and send it forth to carry the message.

Dancing the power animal

Just as is the case with soul retrievals, power animal retrievals almost always require certain rituals to be performed following the journey. In core shamanism, following the retrieval of the animal, and after the energy has been introduced into the person, the person is asked to 'dance' the animal. This is done immediately after the journey and at times may be required to be performed for several days following the journey. If the ritual is not performed the power animal energy might leave again. In fact, if we were to adopt shamanism as a way of life, it is recommended for us to dance our power animals on a regular basis. There are other ways in which we can maintain a relationship and a connection with our power animals as well. One of these is to be aware of our significant dreams and to recognise the possible messages that our power animal may be conveying to us through them.

Amongst the Karinia the meaning of the word *Uba* is both 'dance' and 'existence'. They consider dance to have, among other powers, the power to create an identity. A dance and a tune may transform people. They believe that when the spirits wish to, by using a dance and a song, they may transform the shape of a person. The Karinia use the expression 'dancing someone', which means to bring a person to dance the dance of another person, and by which the owner of the dance becomes the owner of the person dancing it. The connotation the Karinia have with this concept is a negative one, since it implies possession of one's soul through the dance and song, but the basic concept is still very much related to the concept of dancing a power animal. By dancing the animal we are embodying and incorporating the essence of the animal into ourselves. Unlike the Karinia concept of dancing *somebody*, the action we take when dancing our power animal is that of embodying the animal energy into ourselves, rather than being possessed by its spirit.[26]

The practice of dancing a power animal is incredibly similar to the Buddhist practice of 'deity yoga'. During this, the yogi experiences themselves as merging with an image of a godlike deity. After merging, the yogi attempts to embody it as fully as possible, speaking, walking and moving as the virtuous godlike figure. The Tibetans regard this practice to be one of the most effective on the path to spiritual enlightenment.[27] Just as the yogi practice is extremely powerful, so is dancing one's power animal or guardian spirit a most empowering experience. This may also indicate to us that relatively modern spiritual practices may have originated in ancient shamanic ones.

DIAGNOSTIC JOURNEYS

In most cases, and especially when the cause or nature of the illness is not obvious, a shaman will embark on a form of diagnostic journey in order to first clarify the nature of the disease and possible healing interventions. This diagnostic procedure may take many different forms, depending on the culture of the shaman as well as the presenting problem.

While the diagnosis requires the shaman to enter the spirit realms and find the reason for the illness, many different means to achieve this have been documented throughout the world. Some shamans go on a full shamanic journey in order to diagnose the reason and possible cure for a disease, and may even attempt to solve the cause of the problem immediately once encountering it. Others may undertake long periods of isolation and contemplation to diagnose the cause of the illness and request advice on how to heal it. One form of divination incorporates the use of stones, bones or seeds of different colours or shapes, others are based on dream interpretations and yet other shamans may simply need to stare into the fire in order to divine the problem they are facing.

One interesting method for diagnosis was recorded by the Danish explorer Knud Rasmussen[28] and is used by the Eskimo shamans. The method involves tying a belt around the ill person's head, presenting questions to the spirits regarding the disease and lifting the person's head, using the belt. The assumption behind this procedure is that the spirits are answering the questions presented by influencing the weight of the person's head. If the answer to the question is affirmative, then the spirits enter the person's head, thus making it extremely heavy and virtually impossible to lift. If the answer to the question is negative, the spirits avoid entering the head, thus making it light and easy to lift. This technique is interestingly similar to the more modern practice of kinesiology, which is based on measuring changes in muscle tension, for diagnostic purposes.

In core shamanic practice we also have a variety of diagnostic procedures which we can employ. Some of these involve diagnosis with the help of the rattle, diagnosis with the help of the spirits of nature, and a diagnostic journey to the upper world in search of teaching and guidance from one's own spirit teachers. Different diagnostic techniques are used depending on the presenting problem. The rattle and spirits of nature may be used for both diagnostic and healing work and are addressed fully later on. A diagnostic journey to the upper world is usually a very helpful and informative tool since during such a journey we receive information not only regarding the nature or causes of the problems but also regarding possible healing interventions.

At times, when there is need, I embark upon a diagnostic journey before discussing the presenting problem or any other detailed information with the person who is seeking help. The accuracy of the diagnosis is always astounding and the messages invariably speak to the person. It is important to note that this is not just my own personal experience but that of other shamanic counsellors. In very rare cases, where a person needs urgent help but cannot come to me for the journey, I may even perform a diagnostic journey from a distance, without prior acquaintance with the person. This is not something I do very often. However, even in these cases, the accuracy of the messages from the spirits is stunning.

Smith,[29] in an attempt to explain the working of shamanic diagnostic journeys from a Jungian perspective, provides us with the following metaphor:

> Imagine that our psyches overlap and interpenetrate one another like the circles of a Venn diagram, and perhaps all our circles are encompassed by a greater circle, the divine reality. Then it is possible for my spirit guide to enter your psyche, or more accurately, it would tune in to your psyche through a shamanic altered state of consciousness. The journey of the shaman would in effect be a tuning in to your frequency, rather than a literal traversing of external space and time. You might even access my spirit guide, and see it in an altered state of consciousness. Even if my spirit guide is a manifestation of the archetypal Self, it is none the less real.

Although shamans would probably use different terminologies in explaining the working of the diagnostic journey, or shamanic journeys in general, Smith's explanation does not stand in any contradiction to the shamanic worldview. The only claim with which the shaman may disagree is that our spirit guide (or guardian spirit) may be a manifestation of the archetypal self rather than an independent spirit essence.

Diagnostic journeys may have powerful healing effects in their own right. From my experience, at times, just by listening to the messages given by the spirits on a diagnostic journey, and prior to any further shamanic work being carried out, some people experience a profound transformation in themselves. Such a case was that of Ophra, a young Israeli woman.

Ophra came to me as an emergency referral and I had no prior knowledge about her before going on the journey. Although her process of healing included further shamanic work, merely listening to the diagnostic journey had a significant impact on her and gave her further hope to continue the work. I present her case here in her own words, and the diagnostic journey I did for her:

> *When I first came to shamanism I had been seven years in therapy, working with a psychologist, twice a week. I was suffering from anxieties and depression; I had suicidal tendencies and fear of losing my sanity. Although the therapy brought issues to my awareness, I didn't know what to do with them or how to put the advice given to me into practice. The fact is that I was getting worse and feeling stuck with the therapy. I came to shamanism when I started to be afraid that I would hurt people. I decided that I needed to do something else, something different, and I started to work with shamanism.*
>
> *The work started with the diagnostic journey. That journey reflected my state so accurately that it shocked me because it made the state in which I was more real, but at the same time it also gave me hope that there is something I can do about it. That was important at that time because I was in a place in my life where I didn't know what I could do any more; I was in a state beyond self-destruction.*

A diagnostic journey for Ophra

I am going on a journey to ask my spirit helpers to tell me where Ophra is at this time in her life and what help she needs. I am in my power place. My guardian spirit is there. I get on his back and we are going up. I feel I can't breathe. 'That is okay, Arvick,' he reassures me. 'She cannot breathe.' We are flying in the sky and we meet Pegasus. I leave my guardian spirit and go on his back. He tells me: 'She is the warrior woman in her soul, but the only war she has is with herself. She wars with herself. She is on a path of self-destruction, slowly killing herself. The warrior. The warrior woman that can move heaven and earth and instead of that she is destroying herself. In her heart she knows that she is that warrior, that capable woman, but she is not able to achieve it.'

We land in front of my teacher. I sit down. He looks a bit angry, walking up and down in front of a blackboard. I feel dizzy with him walking like that. He is going really fast up and down, looking very thoughtful. I see an image. It's like a rocky mountain, very classic, pointed, a rocky mountain that looks like a tipi, like it has the entrance of a tipi. It's carved. Inside it is dark and hollow. It's a rocky mountain, it's very strong, it's really powerful, but it has an arched entrance, a hole in it and it is dark inside. My teacher tells me:

'Yes. That is Ophra. There is a specific strength in this woman that keeps her alive, that keeps her going. She is that rocky mountain, but she is incomplete, hollow, she has lost so much energy. She is only surviving on the reserves of the rocky mountain that she is, on the reserves of her power. She is capable of doing anything; losing her mind, destroying people and things. She is so lost, so lost. She is eaten from the inside, eaten the strength out of this rocky mountain. Only

a shell left to keep her going. We are not very happy with this situation. She is killing herself.'

Now he is showing me another mountain, like a twin, without the hole. It is very strong, very solid, shiny, and beautiful, with lots of vegetation at the bottom of it. All around it is greenery, beautiful colourful little flowers and some trees. He tells me:

'Yes. That is also her. That is what she was born to be. But the self-destruction in her has turned her into that mountain. No vegetation, nothing growing around it, and it is hollowed, it is eaten, it's just an empty shell of a rock, just something that barely keeps her alive. And if she is not careful, she will dig into that and will totally destroy herself. She is on a self-destruct path. That is where she is at. She is very sophisticated, she destroys herself from inside. And outside she does everything to appear as if she is taking care of herself.'

He is showing me a tiny little girl, around 2 or 3 years old.

'It started from that age. She is such a bright person, very intelligent. And that is the other thing; her intelligence is part of her self-destruction. Because she is so clever, she knows how to do it, she knows how to cover up. She is too intelligent, but the soul inside her, the healthy part of her, is every so often nudging her – hey, wake up, Ophra, don't kill me. And then she gets into panic and goes to do some bandaging job, and then she reverts back. This time, it's a warning. This mountain will not stand forever. This is a warning. She really has got to take herself seriously. Her time has not come to die. But there are so many different ways to die. She is killing her soul as well as her body, destroying herself.'

'What is the reason she is doing this?' I ask him.

'We are not interested in why people get the way they are. That is history. We are interested in how to heal and move on and have a healthy life. She has suffered traumas, like all; traumas and messages that are destroying her. She has belief systems beyond belief. Her belief systems are destroying her. She needs to heal them.'

'But can Ophra become the other mountain you showed me? You talk in a way that frightens me.'

'I would never show you an image if it was not possible to achieve it. Of course she can be that mountain again. It is in her. That is her. That is her soul. That is her life mission, to become that strong mountain, with vegetation, with beauty, and to shine and to be proud and happy and solid.'

'The image is so sad; I don't like to look at it. It makes me feel very sad,' I tell him.

'Well, what do you think she feels? She lives that image. She is that mountain, with a hole in it, eaten away. Imagine rock to be eaten away. Imagine how powerful and sophisticated she is to destroy herself. She also has that power to build herself up. If she can do one, she can do the other. We would like to help her to achieve that. She is very low. She is at her lowest ebb, capable of destruction, destroying others and herself; capable of anything, absolutely anything. You need to hear her story; you need to hear her pain. She needs to be heard and listened to. Take this little soul back with you; take this 3-year-old back. It will give her some energy. She needs more than that, but it will just give her that extra energy, to just barely keep her going.'

I talk to the little girl and ask her to come with me. She agrees. I take the soul. My teacher tells me:

'This will only give her a little bit of life. Not much. She is too weak. She is just a very thin layer of rock. You see, the hole is just getting bigger and bigger and inside it becomes shallower and shallower. So this soul will just give her a little bit of boost. She needs to have confidence, she needs to believe in herself. She has got to work with this self-sabotage, the self-destruct in her; she needs to work with that. She deserves to live, she deserves to be happy, because she is a very beautiful, loving person. She deserves the best. Her fears show themselves up in her questioning. She questions everything. Her depression comes out in the form of questioning things, being sceptical. She is tired.

Now he is showing me Ophra outside the mountain, with energy oozing out of her hands. 'What are you trying to tell me?' I ask him.

'The energy work she is doing is the only thing that is keeping her going. But it cannot continue to support her if she does not work with her issues. We would like to help her. She needs power animals, to strengthen her, to be able to cope with the future souls that she will need. She needs a power animal to help her to believe in herself, to believe she is that mountain. She needs to journey and find out what are the payoffs of her self-destructive behaviour. She needs to look at her fears. And then we will instruct you further. We are very concerned for this woman. You have come at the right time. There is a lifetime of work in what I have given you. She will understand what I am talking about. She can become that mountain. She needs to do the work, to totally commit herself to herself. I am done. You can go now.'

The drums are calling me back. I bow to my teacher, go back with Pegasus. We meet my guardian spirit and I go on his back. We return.

Ophra continued to work shamanically. She went on a beginners' course on shamanism and had three private sessions of shamanism, in addition to working with breath work both privately and on a course. This is her own account as to the effects the work had on her life:

The metaphor of the two mountains in the diagnostic journey had a great impact on me and helped me realise where I truly was in my life. I built models of the two mountains; one black mountain that was hollowed and one green mountain with flowers at the bottom of it. When I finished working on them, I kept them in my home and kept looking at them, reminding myself of the messages the spirits gave me on the journey. One day I couldn't look at them any more, I was done with them, and I just put them away.

I also started to work shamanically myself. One of the biggest realisations I had was on a journey I did to ask what was my fear of losing my sanity trying to teach me. I realised from that journey that dwelling on issues of losing my mind and other fears I had were giving my life meaning and content. I had always felt that life had no meaning, that there is no reason to live, since we all die at the end. Following the journey my fears lessened and I realised I had more charge over my life and my choices.

In the short term, the work helped me to be more active in dealing with my issues. I always thought that I could heal myself through others and that I depended on others. Through my shamanic work I understood that I need to do the work myself, that it needs to come from me. In the long term, I have changed my work place, I have better relationships with people in my life and I went out to the world instead of eating myself from inside. Before, I didn't trust myself to talk or stand in front of people. Now, I am standing in front of students in classes, I talk to people, I have gained back my vitality and life. Today I am more in charge of my life and more in contact with my own power. Fears are still there but I have more power and tools to confront them.

RATTLE HEALING

We have already discussed at length the importance of the rattle in shamanic work in Chapter 3. Just like the drum, the rattle is used primarily to help us enter into an altered state of consciousness and transports us to the spirit realms. The rattle also has other uses in shamanic work. As mentioned before, it may be used for diagnostic purposes. The rattle, or rather the spirits of the rattle, can also be used in shamanic healing work.

Among the Kalinia the rattle is known to be a powerful shamanic tool. It is made of a dry gourd and perforated with holes of different sizes. Seeds and small stones are inserted into the rattle, as well as four larger stones, which symbolise the spirits of the ancestors. According to the Kalinia shaman, it is these four stones or ancestral spirits that are the true voice of the rattle, while the smaller stones and seeds are the servants of these four powerful spirits. Since these servants are many, the shaman addresses some of them during each healing ceremony, depending on the type of the disease and its severity.

In order to invoke the healing powers of the rattle, the shaman must first fill it up with smoke. The shaman smokes the tobacco, then blows it into the rattle through the holes in the gourd. When the rattle is filled the shaman begins to shake it and sing. The smoke, the rattling and the singing attract the spirits to the rattle. They then enter the rattle and settle inside it. The rattle becomes their home and the shaman gains the powers of these spirits to use for healing.[30]

I believe this demonstrates one of the most important points regarding the rattle. That is, although the rattle helps us to enter an altered state of consciousness (ASC) through its rhythmic sound, as well as heal various illnesses, it is not the noise the rattle produces that has healing effects, but rather the spirits which reside within and guide the shaman and facilitate the healing. In core shamanic practices, prior to starting to use the rattle for diagnostic or healing purposes, we would go on a journey to meet the spirit of the rattle.

The rattle is most effective in accessing and releasing blocked energy. This is beautifully demonstrated in a case my teacher Jonathan Horwitz once experienced, of working with the rattle for healing purposes:

A woman contacted me because she was 'blocked'. Could I help her to open these 'blockages'? 'Blockages' was not a term in my shamanic diagnostic vocabulary at the time. I had no idea what she was talking about, but I trusted that my spirits would know what was going on. So I replied that I didn't know if I could help her, but why not come over and we'd see what we could do. When I asked my spirits, they said, 'Use your rattle.' So after calling to the spirits I began to rattle over her body. She began to shake, more and more violently, and then to convulse. The part of me that was in ordinary reality began to be quite alarmed. I asked my spirits what was going on, and was told to shut up, pay attention, and keep rattling. Finally with a roaring-barking sound, she heaved one final huge convulsion and something left her body, flying out of her mouth and out of the opened window. She sighed a sigh of relief and asked me what I'd done. I quite honestly replied that I just shook the rattle and it took care of the rest.[31]

HEALING FROM SPIRITS OF NATURE

Just as shamans believe that we are related to animals, they also believe that we are related to nature; that we are connected with nature, on some deep level of our existence. People of shamanic cultures have a deep respect for all that is alive, and recognise the life which sparks within everything that surrounds us – be it animal, plant or seemingly inanimate elements. Even today, in the industrial and technological world in which we live, people that connect with spirituality through shamanism also come to experience a deep connection with nature, and acquire a sense of respect for all inhabitants of this planet.

The fact is that the spirits of nature are more accessible to us than we may realise. We can all speak to the spirits of nature in search for advice or healing. Unfortunately, most of us have become disconnected with nature. One of the teachings given to me by Moses, one of my spirit teachers, touches on that fact and the implications it has for our lives.

This particular spirit teacher usually uses metaphors and images from nature in his teachings. He advised me to address our relationship with nature in this book:

> *Talk about nature, about how I use nature in forms of symbols and metaphors, to help you understand my messages. And we use those because nature speaks to you, because you under-*

stand it, it's simple; because basically humans and nature ought to live side by side in harmony. The disconnection from the nature has created a deep loneliness and isolation. You have lost the way, you people. You have built your world with concrete. You have killed the nature and turned it into dead concrete. And plastics. You are yearning for contact with nature again. With the magic, with the wisdom. Your science is not taking you very far. It's righting one thing and spoiling another. But that's the process you have to go through.

Since the shaman considers everything to have life and spirit, so in search for knowledge and healing we may also approach the spirit teachers that reside within trees, rocks, water, plants and all that exists in nature. While in an altered state of consciousness the shaman can actually communicate directly with these spirits of nature, approaching them with respect, delicacy and humbleness.

In core shamanic practices, there are a variety of ways in which the shamanic counsellor can communicate with the spirits of nature for healing purposes. One of those is by journeying for a power plant. Such a journey begins by going out to nature, with a mission in mind, and with the willingness to receive a teaching from any plant which might attract the person's attention and call them. The shamanic counsellor would then approach it, observe it from all aspects and sides and begin to converse with its spirit. They would then ask permission from the plant to take a part of it away from nature with them. Having received the messages and the spirit's permission, the shamanic counsellor would embark on a journey to meet and converse with the spirit aspect of the plant.

One such journey I once did was for Paul, a 49-year-old American man who was diagnosed with brain cancer. When I did the diagnostic journey for him I was instructed to speak to the spirits of nature and ask for help. Paul was finding it extremely difficult to open up and talk about himself, his emotions and his illness in general. The messages from the journey I did to the spirits of nature not only gave him hope, but the confidence and assurance he needed to open up and speak. The following are some of the significant messages given to me by the spirits of nature for Paul:

On this journey, I met a bush with red berries, growing on the side of a hill. It told me:

> *Look at me. In spite of all the weeds around me, that draw energy, I am standing – colourful, strong, and going with the season. The reason the weeds do not affect me is because I am in my power. Because in spite of all the elements around me, that are, I allow them to be who they are, what they are. I am me, they are them. I don't allow them to take energy and deplete my roots. And they don't allow me to take energy from them and deplete their roots. In nature, we all complement one another and survive, and live and grow. Each one of us is different and has its own quality, its own beauty. And we are happy and satisfied with who we are and what we are, what we look like, and what pleasure we give to the world. Each one of us, in its own right, is admired and appreciated. We have no competition here. In nature, we are happy with who we are. Therefore, each one of us is noticed, in its own right. Not everybody likes us. Some people like*

me and admire my beauty. Others walk past me and admire the plant or the tree next to me. We understand that.

I next met a bush with tiny white flowers. It spoke to me:

Look at me, look at the condition in which I am growing, among rocks, on a straight wall. Some would say 'impossible'. Nothing is impossible. We can survive in any circumstances. It is not my circumstances that are creating the survival. It is my own will. My roots are strong enough to penetrate the rocks. That is my message for Paul. He is strong enough to penetrate the rocks. He can survive anything. When he believes in himself, and when he comes to truly understand that. But he needs to be willing to live differently, to be an individual, to connect with his spirituality, be the beautiful person that he is. And not be affected by the fears of his family and surroundings. When Paul is ready to work with his fears and let go, then he will be like me, he will survive anything. Take me with you and let him listen to my messages. Paul, you are stronger than you have ever imagined. You are capable of penetrating rocks, like me. Your roots are strong. Nurture your soil and nurture yourself. Deep from your heart, be willing to help yourself and the help will be there for you.

Although the messages on this journey did not directly address Paul's state of health or illness, it seems that they address some of the deep issues that he needed to deal with at the time. These messages actually helped Paul to open up and talk about his illness and the hardships he was experiencing at the time with his family and himself. He also realised how the issues addressed by the spirits on the journey had always hindered both his working and social life.

Another form in which we can receive guidance, healing or help from the spirits of nature is simply by going out and seeking it. As is the case in all shamanic work, we must first establish in our minds the problem or question we are facing. We then go out to nature, with our mission in mind, and allow anything in nature to attract us or call us. After encountering our spirit teacher we then sit with the plant or object and put the issue to it, writing down any messages given. In this technique no further journeying to meet the spirit aspect of the plant is necessary.

A very ancient and more specific technique exists among the North American Indians. A person seeking the help of a shaman would choose a large rock and bring it to the shaman. The shaman would then instruct the person to carefully observe the stone from all sides and aspects and, while holding his question or problem in mind, describe the images seen upon the rock. After all the images of the rock have been described by the person, the shaman proceeds by asking them to describe how the images are clarifying, explaining or enlightening their problem or concern. The shaman then provides their own images and understandings.[32] The combination of the messages is used to help the person to have a clearer understanding of their situation or may even provide a solution to their presenting problem.

* * *

Crazy Woman

Don't craze far to find the truth

Stay in your heart

Dance at different tempos

Through the seasons of your life

To heal your heart To die, to live...

Autumn 2003

6 The Magic of Shamanism: The Journey as a Vehicle for Transformation

Image is the language of the soul.
Aristotle

In the year 1987 I was offered a job in New York, working for a centre that was working with families and children. This offer came at a time in my life when I was going through a crisis. Trying to escape my own emotions, I grabbed the opportunity, left England and went to New York. The work culture in New York was very different from that I had experienced in the UK. For the first eight months I felt like a fish out of water, trying to integrate myself and failing at it. I was judging myself and trying to force myself into changing and fitting in to my new surroundings. At the time I was also studying NLP and one of the units was looking at therapeutic stories and learning how to construct them according to a person's presenting problem.

My teacher was aware of my inner struggles at that time and suggested that I tell my story and that the whole class, including herself, would create a metaphor to help me with my situation. Although all stories were interesting and affected me to some degree, it was the teacher's story which affected me most, and which literally changed the course of my working life in America. This was her story.

Once upon a time, there was a beautiful bird that lived peacefully on an island. She had lots of friends and knew *her surroundings very well; she knew where to look for food and how to survive. She had lots of friends and family. Then, one day, there was a big storm, that carried her away from the familiar island. She was lost, but eventually landed on another island.*

The birds on this island were very different-looking. The food supply was different and the bird felt an outsider and considered herself ugly and strange. Because of those feelings, she was withdrawn and shy, unable to mix, and felt very lonely, miserable and unhappy. She did not know how to find her way back home.

One day, the bird was walking by a river, feeling very sad and lonely. Suddenly she felt thirsty and approached the river to drink. Bending down, she noticed a reflection in the water. The reflection was that of a very beautiful bird. Shocked and surprised, she looked around to see whose image she was seeing in the water. There was no one there. She looked again in the river, and the same image appeared. It was by the third time that suddenly she realised the image she was seeing was in fact her own reflection.

The bird understood she had forgotten her own beauty. This gave her a great deal of confidence and helped her to become more sociable, mix and talk and acquire many friends. She was happy with her new friends and they soon helped her to find the way back to her island, back to her home.

This story had a tremendous effect on me. I cannot explain how, but I became very much connected with my power. I became aware of my abilities and my strengths, I found myself, I returned home to myself. At the time I was also offered a position in Arizona, which I was debating whether to take or not. It was this story that helped me to take the right decision, which changed the course of my life. This metaphor was one of the most truly powerful therapies I had ever experienced, up until then; and it has stayed with me ever since. I carry it with me wherever I go and it still continues to help me today, in situations and times where I am lost.

Now that we are familiar with the shaman's world, and have explored the techniques of shamanic healing, we reach the inevitable question – how does it work? How do shamans heal, or rather, how do the spirits heal? How can we explain the magic of shamanic journeys?

There are many possible answers to these questions. In order to answer them, let us begin by further exploring the means by which the spirits communicate with us during the shamanic journey. In other words, let us explore the language of shamanic journeys, the language of the spirits, the language of our very soul.

THE POWER OF IMAGERY

The ability to 'image' or engage in mental imagery appears to be a capacity with which we are all born.[1] Images and imagery are the immediate medium of shamanic journeys. We shall now explore the healing power and mechanisms of imagery work in general, as it is used in different forms of therapy today.

Jeanne Achterberg,[2] in her book *Imagery in Healing*, thoroughly reviews the history of western medicine and traces the use of imagery in the healing arts all the way back to Ancient Greece. Up until the Renaissance, healers and doctors believed that the mind, the body and the spirit were inseparable and took a holistic approach to healing. It was only following the birth of the Cartesian model of dualism and the separation between the mind and the body that the holistic approach could no longer logically exist within the context of healing.

The mind or soul was now viewed as a separate entity, existing independently of the physical body. What followed was a separation – the medical doctor was now in charge of the body, while the priest was in charge of the soul. This gave doctors permission to invade the human body, to explore, examine and dissect it without fear of any damage to the person's soul. The downside to this process was the fact that the image and imagery work lost their credibility and status within the medical profession. The imagination, clearly a manifestation of the human soul, could no longer be regarded to have any relation to the physical body, and thus any relation to healing and medicine.

Since the days of Descartes, and until recently, imagery held a peripheral position within mainstream medicine. In the last few decades, however, practices based on imagery work have gained popularity and credibility within the western medical establishment. Although these techniques are still not occupying a central position within mainstream medicine, they are nevertheless credited as useful tools for improving the psychological well-being of ill people.

Whether acknowledged or not, imagery holds a most central albeit somewhat hidden role in all medical practices. We are always imagining, whether we are aware of it or not. When a situation is described to us, we all automatically form an image of that situation in our minds, in order to make sense of the explanation we are given. All human interactions are accompanied by human imagining.

Thus, for example, when we are informed by the doctor that we are suffering from a certain affliction, immediately an image is formed in our minds, depicting that particular physical problem described by the doctor. That image, and the images that come to mind following it, whether they be negative or positive, will affect our physical body and the course of our healing to a large degree. Reports appear in medical literature of either miraculous healings in cases where the patient was diagnosed with a terminal illness, or alternatively cases in which a feared diagnosis given by a doctor caused almost instant death for no apparent medical reasons.

While the power of images to bring about healing is not yet fully acknowledged by the mainstream medical world, imagery work is to be found in relative abundance in the psychological sphere. The therapeutic value of images is widely acknowledged by therapists of different traditions. The effectiveness of hypnosis, for example, is considered by many hypnotherapists to lie in the images created by the person as a result of the hypnotic suggestion. Many other schools of therapy make explicit use of images and imagery work in order to bring about therapeutic transformation and healing. These include Jungian therapy, Gestalt work, art therapy, biofeedback and numerous others.

When referring to imagery work, we need to be clear that not only the visual but also other sensory systems are very likely to be involved in the process. For example, while visualising, people may also hear, feel, sense, smell or taste things.

The evidence as to the effects of the image on the physical body are many and fascinating. It is clear from numerous practices and evidence gathered in research that the image has a direct as well as indirect, powerful influence on the body and its processes. It appears that 'no thought fails to leave a corporeal mark; no neurochemical signal occurs without being registered by the mind'.[3]

IMAGERY AND SHAMANISM

As we have seen, imagery work is most effective in creating change on a physical and mental level. It has been and still is widely used both in western medicine and psychological practice. Let us now explore the role of imagery in the context of the shamanic journey.

Certainly, one of the most popular claims of many researchers in the field of shamanism is that the shamanic journey is not a journey to the realms of the spirits, but rather an exploration of the depths of our own unconscious mind. Many consider the shamanic journey to be a form of visualisation work. Carl Jung actually conducted shamanic journeys and called the process 'active imagination'.* In one of his books he tells of the process which led him to the discovery of the technique. As he was sitting at his desk and considering his fears he decided to take a significant step: 'I let myself drop. Suddenly it was as though the ground literally gave way beneath my feet, and I plunged down into the darkest depths.'[4] Jung's experience of plunging into the depths is extremely similar to the shaman's descent into the lower world. In his processes of active imagination, Jung would descend down a dark passage until he arrived in another world.

---

* A process of active imagination involves calling a fictitious image into the mind and conducting a dialogue of a sort with it. For example, if I have a problem, I would call an image to my mind that symbolises that problem or an aspect of that problem and proceed to talk to it, and write the dialogue. This would or could continue over a prolonged period of time, with breaks in between.

Many people on my courses also claim, believe or fear that their own shamanic journeys are 'nothing but' their imagination. Personally, I believe that when we are truly journeying shamanically we are no longer within the confines of our own mind and imagination, but rather traversing the realms of the spirits. However, it is not possible, and perhaps never will be possible, to assert whether a spirit realm exists or whether we are merely traversing our own unconscious mind (be it our private or collective one) (see Chapter 4).

As I said earlier, a great variety of therapeutic techniques make use of imagery work. These are most commonly referred to as techniques of visualisation or guided imagery. The question arises, then, what is the difference between the large range of therapeutic techniques which make use of imagery or visualisation and the shamanic journey?

While it is clear that some commonality exists between these techniques and shamanic journeying, there is also a significant difference between them. In the case of guided imagery, it is the therapist who constructs the framework of the visualisation, while the client only fills in the gaps. Another point to consider is that in visualisation work the person visualising consciously makes use of the imagination to call certain images to mind. In contrast, when one embarks on a shamanic journey all one is provided with is the drum beat as the means to enter an ASC. The imagination or the skill of visualisation only comes into play during the period before the journey starts (when the journeyer calls the power place to mind). In fact, the key to successful journeying is to let go and enter the journey without any assumptions or preconceptions as to what is about to happen.

People who have gone on a shamanic journey often express surprise and wonder at their experiences during the journey. At times they would even go on a journey with certain expectations as to what they may see or hear, and yet would invariably have thoroughly different experiences.

Another difference between shamanic journeys and imagery work is that while techniques of guided imagery may involve meeting teachers or entities for healing or teaching purposes, the process does not involve a significant alteration of the state of consciousness that happens in shamanic journeys.

One other therapeutic technique which does involve a significant alteration of the state of consciousness is hypnosis. While under hypnotic suggestion a person may experience travelling to other realms and even believe in their realness, just as is the case with the shamanic journey. However, a significant difference lies in the fact that the shaman or shamanic journeyer does not receive any guidance or suggestion from an outside source, as is the case with the process of hypnosis. The shaman does not require another person to assist them in inducing the ASC or in directing their journey through the spirit realms by the use of suggestion. Rather, the shaman enters and traverses the spirit worlds at will.

METAPHORS

Just as the spirits talk to us with images, so they talk to us with metaphors and symbols. Shamanic journeys as reported by shamans of numerous cultures are imbued with symbology and metaphors. Both are ancient tools for communication and are most effective in bringing about transformation. In this section we explore the meaning of metaphors in both the therapeutic and shamanic context.

What is a metaphor?

Metaphor by its nature is a flexible term. The Collins dictionary, for example, defines a metaphor as 'a figure of speech in which a word or phrase is applied to an object or action that it does not literally denote in order to imply a resemblance'. This definition of metaphor is a rather narrow one. From experience we have learned that metaphors may appear in more forms that just 'a figure of speech'. Aristotle, for example, provided us with a broader definition. According to him, 'Metaphor consists in giving the thing a name that belongs to something else; the transference being either from genus to species or from species to species or on the grounds of analogy'.[5]

According to this definition we can conclude that many other narrative forms, such as allegory, myth, parables and fables, can all serve as metaphors. In the therapeutic sphere the term 'metaphor' has been given a very broad meaning. Long stories, objects and activities may contain metaphorical meanings and be used successfully in therapy.

Metaphors have been used to convey messages indirectly throughout human history. We must assume, then, that great advantages lie in communicating messages in metaphorical means rather than directly. We shall now explore the power that metaphors have to bring about transformation and healing and the way in which they are used in the therapeutic context. We will then continue to explore the relationship between metaphors and shamanic journeys. Since metaphors are often presented, especially in the therapeutic context, in the form of stories, I will at times refer to metaphors as stories.

Metaphors and transformation

Metaphors and stories can be used in the therapeutic setting for a variety of purposes. The counsellor or therapist may use a metaphor for such ends as making or illustrating points, suggesting solutions to problems, helping people to recognise themselves, seeding ideas and increasing motivation.

What are the specific advantages of using metaphors in therapy? First, a well-constructed and well narrated story, presented at the appropriate time, can illuminate and inspire ideas and solutions which the person we work with had not considered in the past. A metaphor can create interest, convey information and messages in a much more powerful and inspiring way than directly stating those same messages. While we can make points directly, a metaphor holds magic, captures the imagination and stimulates creative thought more effectively than a direct instruction would. A story by its nature implies possibilities, movement and change. In the same way that the characters of a story may change, a story might communicate the possibility of transformation and growth to the listener.

Secondly, stories and metaphors are, by nature, less threatening or confronting than direct messages. If a therapist makes a suggestion directly there is a chance that the client, weighing the suggestion in their mind, will end up consciously rejecting it. In this case, there is also a risk of the therapeutic relationship being compromised. On the other hand, while listening to a story, the client has the choice to either internalise and accept the messages embedded in it, or reject them, if they are not yet ready to deal with the issue.

However, messages embedded within stories are more often accepted than rejected, exactly because they are not direct. While a story of any kind may be perceived literally on a conscious level, its metaphoric content may register on an unconscious level. Another point to consider is that a story may be perceived as metaphorical regardless of the storyteller's intention in the first place.

This touches on a very important point regarding metaphorical work in therapy. The use of metaphors relocates the locus of responsibility for change from the therapist to the client. Exactly because a metaphor, by nature, is ambiguous rather than direct or clear, it encourages both deep listening and self-searching within the person who listens to it.

The use of metaphor also frees the therapist from having to provide explanations or interpretations regarding the person's present issues. Instead, it is the client's responsibility and option to assign their own personal interpretation to the metaphor presented. Hence, within the therapeutic relationship, the locus of power is subtly shifted towards the client. In a very subtle way, this asserts the notion that it is the client who creates change in their lives, rather than the therapist.

Metaphors, words, stories or ideas in general have been believed for generations to facilitate healing on physical, psychological or spiritual levels. Indeed, scientific evidence does exist to imply a relationship between physiological response and narratives. Gold[6] suggested that reading a story may produce a physiological reaction similar to that of experiencing a parallel life event. It appears that essentially the same neural signals manifest throughout our nervous system in both cases. If merely listening to a story can bring about transformation within us, then surely experiencing a live story during a shamanic journey could bring about an even greater change.

Some evidence exists implying a possible neurological basis for the effectiveness of metaphor. It appears that a certain division of labour exists between the right and left brain hemispheres, concerning information processing. While the left brain specialises in processing the literal, sequential and logical aspects of language, the right brain processes the structural, kinaesthetic, Gestalt and metaphorical ones. It appears that therapies which address the right brain directly, such as those which make use of metaphors, stories or hypnotherapy, produce faster results than therapies which address the left brain primarily:[7]

> There are thus two languages involved. The one, in which for instance this sentence itself is expressed, is objective, definitional, cerebral, logical, analytic; it is the language of reason, of science, explanation and interpretation, and therefore the language of most psychotherapy. The other . . . is much more difficult to define – precisely because it is not the language of definition. We might call it the language of imagery, of metaphor, perhaps of symbols, but certainly of synthesis and totality, and not of analytical dissection.[8]

Shamanic journey and metaphors

Using metaphors and stories may be very effective in the therapeutic setting, but creating the right one is a challenging task. Indeed, if it's the wrong one, a metaphor can be just as powerfully harming as it can be helpful. Even if the metaphor is not harming, it can still be ineffective if not constructed and used correctly. Many considerations have to be taken into account by a therapist when attempting to construct a metaphor or therapeutic story. Identifying the person's problem, the choice of visual, auditory or kinesthetic modality* which would be most suitable for the person, the actual words and symbologies that need to be used, and the actual delivery of the metaphor in terms of tone of speech, are just a few of the considerations that need to be taken.

For a metaphor to be effective it must speak to the person. As mentioned before, we all communicate ourselves through stories. It was found that in cases of a good-outcome therapy, therapists had successfully adopted and used metaphor phrases which were initially introduced by the client, while in the cases of poor-outcome therapy, a lack of metaphorical theme within and across sessions was evident.[9] We can see, then, the absolute importance for the therapist to be able to speak the person's language, in therapy in general, but especially when working with stories and metaphors. Without the common language, therapy is not facilitated.

---

* The effectiveness of a metaphor is very much dependent upon the modality used for its delivery. A *modality* is a sensory preference for the receipt and communication of language. The three major modalities are the visual, auditory and kinesthetic. Most people show a distinct preference to one of these modalities over the others, both in communicating and responding to communication. People who show preference for the visual modality would respond best to physical and linguistic cues which are related to the sense of sight. These people would tend to use words such as *look, observe* and *watch* and phrases such as *I see your point, I saw red* etc. People who function within the auditory modality, on the other hand, would tend to respond better to communication related to sound and the hearing sense and would be more prone to use words such as *hear, speak, sound, dialogue* or phrases such as *I hear you*, or *the penny dropped for me*. Persons who operate through the kinesthetic modality are more prone to use words related to the affective world of feelings. They would use words such as *grasp, touch, feel, sense* or phrases such as *I feel this is right or I sense something is wrong*.[10]

This does not apply, of course, to shamanic work. In the process of shamanic counselling, the counsellor is not a mediator between the person and the spirits, and thus is not the facilitator of the healing. Rather, the journeyer comes into direct contact with their own spirit helpers. Since the metaphors, stories and images which appear in the journey are not mediated by the counsellor, they invariably speak to the journeyer because the spirit helpers draw on the person's own world of content and languaging.

All the hurdles standing in the way of the therapist while attempting to construct the appropriate metaphor are literally irrelevant in the case of shamanic counselling. Whether we believe that the metaphors and symbolism spring out of our own unconscious mind, or whether it is our spirit teachers and helpers that speak to us during the journey – the fact still stands that the metaphors are invariably accurate, applicable to the presenting problem and the person's world of content.

Furthermore, since the metaphors in journeys are received by the person while in a deep ASC, their effect is even further enhanced than it would be were they hearing them while in an ordinary state of consciousness (OSC). This issue will be covered in depth later on in this chapter, when we try to understand the power of shamanic journeys to heal.

At this point it is important to note that metaphors, whether in ancient times or today, do not appear in shamanic journeys solely in a verbal or narrative form. Although people may be given metaphoric stories by their spirit teachers, metaphors may also appear in the form of images. During the journey people may also experience certain things or perform certain actions which are in fact metaphorical to some aspect of their lives or problem. For example, one woman who went looking for her guardian spirit found herself extremely confused by its behaviour. Throughout the journey it kept changing shape, from a swan to a duck, a pelican, a goose and other birds. At the time of the journey she felt confused and frustrated with the bird changing its shape constantly. When she returned from the journey, she realised that in her life she did the same. She recognised that she was presenting herself very differently to different people at different times and that this behaviour confused and frustrated people around her. She understood that her guardian spirit was trying to tell her to simply be herself and consequently came to explore this issue in her life and work with it.

It is also possible for an entire journey to constitute a single metaphor. A young man went on a journey to ask what his anxieties and fears were trying to teach him. During the journey, he came across three different teachers. In all encounters the teachers were lively and colourful and the surroundings likewise. However, as soon as he posed his question, the teacher and the scene around the teacher would immediately freeze and turn to ice. This process was repeated with all the teachers he encountered during this journey.

He returned very angry and frustrated, and totally confused, saying that the journey was a complete waste of time. I must admit that at the time I shared his feelings. I was also very confused and didn't understand what had happened during the journey. However, I suggested we listen to the recorded journey together. As we were listening to the story, he suddenly hit his forehead with the palm of his hand and exclaimed loudly, 'Oh, my God. I understand!' His understanding was that his teachers were trying to tell him in the journey that his anxiety and fears were not really teaching him anything. Rather, that they only froze him and disabled him from doing many things in life. A month later we met. He told me that his way of approaching fearful situations was very different, that situations which in the past he considered scary no longer seemed as such any more and that he felt he had let go of some of his most limiting fears and anxieties.

In order to truly understand the way metaphors are used in shamanic journeys, as well as gain a clearer understanding of the working of the shamanic journey in general, I shall now present a full case study of Daniel, a person who attended my shamanic course for beginners and who was interviewed by me a few months later.

DANIEL

Daniel was born, brought up and is currently living in Israel. He is the oldest of three siblings, married with one son who is 3 years old. Daniel is a musician and has his own production company, which was in great financial difficulty at the time he began shamanic counselling work. His psychologist referred him to my breath integration course, suffering from asthma and anxiety attacks accompanied by chest pains, which resulted in rushing him to hospital at least twice a week. He was also using soft drugs on a frequent basis and although he was not very happy about his continued use of drugs, he felt they helped him to escape his fears and feelings of anxiety. After the seven days of the breath integration course, his anxiety attacks lessened and he stopped using soft drugs. Shortly after the course he developed a severe rash, which covered his entire body with the exception of his face. This condition lasted for eight to nine months, during which time he went to see a homeopath, a Chinese doctor and medical doctors (who ran many different tests to try and discover the cause of his condition). All reassured him that he was not suffering from any kind of allergy, but at the same time were not able to diagnose the problem and provide appropriate treatment. The doctors' inability to provide an explanation resulted in strong feelings of frustration and desperation. Due to his positive experience on the breath integration course, Daniel decided to come on a basic shamanic course, led by me.

Journeys one and two – in search of the guardian spirit

The purpose of the first journey Daniel did on the course was to meet his guardian spirit. In this journey, although he succeeded in entering the lower world, Daniel was not able to remain in an ASC for the entire duration of the journey. Even though he met his guardian spirit (an eagle), he did not communicate with it nor recognise it as his guardian spirit and thus did not return back with him. He also had two short interactions with men on the journey. After asking for help from an old man with a pipe, he was directed to the top of a mountain where he was told he would meet his guardian spirit. On his way up the mountain Daniel was helped by the eagle, who carried him to the top of the mountain to a place that looked like a bar. There, he met a strange man with a twisted face, half drunk. Daniel had a strong angry reaction towards this man, who then also cursed him and told him that he was 'nobody, and worth nothing'.

Not having returned with the guardian spirit, Daniel was besieged by feelings of worthlessness and felt he had failed himself. At this point I advised him to journey for a power animal that would give him confidence to trust his experiences on his journeys. In this journey Daniel managed to communicate with his spirit teachers. He met an owl who confirmed that he was his power animal for confidence, and also the eagle that had appeared in his first journey, who confirmed that he was Daniel's guardian spirit.

However, Daniel's first two journeys did not live up to his expectations. He had come to the course with hopes of an immediate solution to his problem (the rash). Following the first two journeys he became extremely disappointed and even considered leaving the course. At the time Daniel was unable to make sense of his experiences and the messages contained in the journeys. However, a year later, when I talked with him about his journeys and their effects, he showed a deep understanding of them, which had helped him to observe and modify some of the negative patterns that influenced his life.

Since Daniel did not have prior experience of shamanic journeying, he was questioning whether his experiences during the journeys were truly shamanic. He thought he was imagining what he was seeing and experiencing. Many people who are new to shamanic journeying tend to question the authenticity of their experience. Often when I ask them what their expectation was, it transpires that they were in fact questioning themselves and their ability to journey. In addition to Daniel's mistrust in his ability to journey, he also had many expectations as to the form in which the communication with the spirits would take place. He expected his guardian spirit to present itself immediately, explain the cause of his rash and provide clear solutions to his problem.

Feelings of frustration, worthlessness and unfulfilled expectations were a repeating theme in Daniel's experiences of his journeys. Even a year after the journeys took place, when I talked with him, almost all of what Daniel was able to remember of his experiences were the feelings and emotions the journeys had evoked in him at that time. Nevertheless, one image and interaction that he recognised as significant and powerful for him from the first two journeys was the encounter with the half-drunk man who cursed him and told him he was worthless. Looking back, Daniel remembered the anger he was feeling towards the drunken man. In his words, 'I was very angry with him. Like, the last thing I needed is someone to tell me what I was already feeling. It was really putting me down, even the way he was looking at me. However, I think that his behaviour and words also were mirroring my own feelings and situation about things.'

Daniel remembered the intense feelings of frustration and anger he felt at that time:

> Well, it was like a strong feeling of being nothing, of being worthless and at the same time feeling very strong resistance and then I rebel against those feelings of nothingness and worthlessness . . . and get stuck in the cage.

Daniel came to recognise that he was in a continuous state of inner war. His unrealistic expectations were serving him by bringing on disappointment and anger in his life, leading him to feelings of extreme low self-worth. These extreme feelings of worthlessness were so overwhelming that they led him, eventually, to rebel against them. It seemed as if Daniel's low self-esteem was so extreme and rendered him so powerless, that he needed to take himself to the depth of that feeling in order to be able to connect with his abilities, inner strength and inner power. It was as if he needed to reach rock bottom, from where the only way out was up.

The inner struggle Daniel described is one taking place between the two polarities on a continuum of self-worth. The half-drunk man in the first journey can be seen as mirroring one end of the continuum, representing the negative, self-denigrating inner voice in Daniel. This negative inner voice was further awakened during the course due to the fact that at the time Daniel believed that he could not journey and was not receiving an immediate answer to his problem.

Daniel concluded that the effects of the first two journeys were to help him observe from a distance his recurring behavioural patterns, hence giving him a deeper understanding of them:

> Yes, it cleared how I work, what are the forces in me, how my mechanism works, where I trigger myself to here and there. To understand the combination of powers in me, the forces of how I bring myself to feelings of nothingness . . . I now see myself, how I go step by step putting all the ingredients [together] and then boom . . .

As is the case in the use of metaphors in therapy, where the metaphor enables the client to step back from their problem, and thus gain a clearer view of it, so it seems that the journeys enabled Daniel to distance himself from his behavioural pattern and free himself from his myopic view of his situation.

Journey three: healing

The mission of this journey was, 'I am going to the lower world, to ask my spirit helpers to give me a healing as they see fit.' The initial mission for the journey was a more specific one. Daniel was about to ask his spirit helpers to give him a healing for his rash. However, when he actually lay down and began to journey he changed his mission. When asked for the reason for phrasing his mission as he did, Daniel could not provide a clear answer. The only explanation he could provide was that since he did not understand his rash, he left it to the spirits to guide and help him as they saw fit. Another explanation could be that since in previous journeys he felt that he did not receive concrete and clear answers, he did not want to set himself up to be disappointed again by hoping or expecting to receive a healing for his rash. It could also be that Daniel, at that time, was still not trusting his ability to journey, based on the experience and understanding he had of his two first journeys.

On this journey, Daniel met his first healer, a knight, who drew a sword and sent a beam of light into his body, in particular into his right side. Daniel's understanding of this action, at the time of the interview, was that the directing of the beam to his right side was connected to his liver. Apparently, the Chinese doctor to whom he went for treatment for his rash had indicated that there was an emotional problem connected to his liver, which was associated with feelings of suppressed anger and was affecting the levels of energy in his body. However, a year later at the time of the interview Daniel appeared very surprised at the realisation and the connection he had made, and said he had not been conscious of this connection immediately after the journey.

Daniel's next experience on the journey was swimming in a river, which led him down two different waterfalls. Going down the waterfalls gave him a nice feeling and he said he was not afraid. During the interview he explained the significance of the waterfalls as having not only a nice, but also a cleansing, effect on him:

> So, it was very much a cleansing. When I'm saying that I don't want to go into the "water is cleansing", I don't want to go there. I know water can clean but it really felt like something clean and pure. It was cleaning me, I felt clean, free and pure.

Daniel was obviously familiar with the popular notion that water is cleansing and he was trying to emphasise that his experience of feeling cleansed by the water during the journey was more than that. The river was not merely a symbol for Daniel – he reported actually experiencing the cleansing effect of the water in his physical body during the journey.

Next, his guardian spirit took Daniel through the desert to somewhere among the stars, where he could see the sun from afar, painted orange. They were standing in mid-air, where it was half light and half darkness. Here he met a magician in a carriage, who invited Daniel to join him. When he asked where he was, the magician replied, 'This is the twilight zone. A place where light and darkness live together.'

Daniel described this experience as being in a state of floating and timelessness. When he asked for a healing the magician told Daniel, 'Your pain is nothing. It's like . . .' – then the magician stretched out his hand, a ball appeared on his head, then it faded and disappeared. Daniel interpreted the symbolic meaning of the magician to be one of high knowledge and wisdom, and the gesture of his hand and the disappearance of the ball from his head to indicate that 'the pain is in my head' (the pain that is referred to is the chest pain Daniel was suffering as a result of his anxiety attacks). This triggered the old feelings of frustration in Daniel, that again the teacher was not giving him a concrete answer or solution to his problem.

From here, the carriage continued to travel on a curved, roller-coaster-like road, hanging in the air. At the end of the road was a palace. For Daniel, this metaphor of the roller-coaster road and the palace at the end of it resembled the narrative outline of a fairy tale:

> I guess for me it is like a fairy tale. It's hard to get there. But there [at the end] is beauty and it's nice.

Bettelheim[11] considers a fairy tale to be therapeutic because through it the client can find their own solution to their problem. In addition, fairy tales, having an unrealistic nature, direct the person's attention to the inner processes which are taking place in them, rather than to their external problems. Although Daniel's presenting problem was physical, the fairy-tale metaphor presented to him in his journey had nothing to do with this external problem. Rather, it dealt with the inner processes that were taking place within him. Daniel saw the roller-coaster road as representing the way he chose to reach the goals in his life – the hard way. He connected the above metaphor with his anxiety-induced chest pains as well as with his feelings of frustration:

> I see a connection . . . it is, in a way, giving me choice. Saying, you can do it . . . Just smooth and easy or you can do it the hard way. And the question that arises for me is why do I choose to always do it the hard way? It feels like it has more worth and it is more honourable if you get something through pain or through long effort . . . and if I work hard to get something then it is worth more than if I get it easily.

In fairy tales, the characters often go through difficulties and trials before reaching a happy ending. Struggle against severe difficulties in life is portrayed in fairy tales as unavoidable, yet holding the promise of future victory and success if one persists with the struggle.[12] It seemed that for Daniel, the palace symbolised his goals in life and the roller-coaster road symbolised the way he achieved them. So, in order to realise his goals, he had to struggle and work hard.

As the journey continued, Daniel entered the palace and walked downward on a beautiful road, feeling very happy. There he met a few playful dwarves. His understanding of the dwarves was that they represented lightness, which was missing in his life:

> Now, looking and listening to the dwarves makes me smile, happy and light . . . That I should not be heavy and serious all the time. Not to dwell on 'I am no good', and if I take it lightly, *'puff'*, the magic will happen. The feeling is that it is more of a choice . . . I can do them in the hard way or I can do them the light and easy way.

Metaphors may contain a set of solutions which direct the person's unconscious mind into generating alternative choices to solve their problem.[13] It seems that for Daniel, the metaphor of the palace and the roller-coaster, followed by the encounter with the dwarves, helped him realise he had choices in his life:

The metaphor of the castle and the roller-coaster road could be regarded as initiating an unconscious process in Daniel, regarding his inner struggle between the two polarities of reaching his goal the hard or easy way. Daniel was connecting this polarity with another polarity in his life – the one of worthlessness and having value for himself. He considered that feelings of low self-esteem were driving him to sabotage himself by doing things the hard way. It is possible that because the first journey triggered feelings of low self-esteem in Daniel, he was then more able to see, through the metaphor of the palace, how his low self- esteem brought him to do things the hard way, which further supported his low self-esteem, trapping him in a vicious cycle of behaviour that did not serve him.

Back on the journey, following his meeting with the dwarves, an elephant arrived and, with his trunk, pumped something from Daniel's heart. Daniel's understanding of the encounter was that it sucked out the sickness from inside him and cleansed him.

Other than perceiving the elephant as a powerful animal, Daniel was interpreting the elephant's action to be concrete and 'real': 'Something was happening. Something practical was happening, it was real.'

This description of his encounter with the elephant is similar to Daniel's earlier description of his cleansing experience in the river. In both cases he described the experiences as 'real' and reported experiencing physical sensations at the time of the journey. These experiences could also be seen as meeting some of Daniel's expectations of receiving a concrete solution to his problems during the journeys.

A few days after the course Daniel's rash disappeared completely and abruptly:

> It was like *'puff'*. . . I remember myself thinking that it can't just go like this. I was thinking to myself before, how nice it would be to start see-

ing the rash going away slowly. And that did not happen. It really was just *'puff '*. . . I woke up one morning and I said, "Wow! It's gone!"

However, although the presenting issue brought to the course was his rash, Daniel also expressed having a much deeper understanding of other issues and how he generally dealt with them in his life. However, Daniel now emphasises that he did not have these understandings of the symbolism and messages contained in the journeys *at the time of the course*, nor immediately after it. In fact, the first time Daniel's understandings and interpretations of his journeys in relation to his life were put into a coherent narrative was during the interview itself, quite some time later. This also demonstrates and stresses the importance of reading our journeys every so often, as this allows us to gain a deeper and more meaningful understanding of the messages embedded in them. From a hermeneutic point of view, human life is a process of narrative interpretation. According to Gadamar,[14] a text is always interpreted in relation to our present situation. Such an application of the text to our present results in a 'fusion of horizons', in which the perspective of the text and of the reader is combined into a new, wider and richer horizon. Gadamar's theory of textual interpretation can be applied to the relation between experience (in this case, experience of the journey) and the story of people's lives. By telling stories about our past experiences, we engage in a process of giving meaning to that experience. According to Gadamar, this requires that we try to see what the experience has to say to us, by applying it to our present situation. In this process, the meaning of the experience is changed, as it is fused with our present understanding. Our life story, in turn, is formed through a process of interpretations of our past, which change the meaning of our life. As it is filled with life experiences, our life story is enriched. Thus it can be said that looking back at his journeys and the metaphors and symbols contained in them, Daniel was now interpreting his journeys in relation to the psychological issues that were present in his life at that time. By this interpretation, he acquired a new and richer understanding of both his life and his experiences during the journeys.

At the end of the interview, looking back at his presenting problem, Daniel saw the rash as one part of a larger picture concerning his life:

> Maybe it was part of a whole – that I do understand. I don't know what specifically the rash was there for, except that it was a signal for something and I reacted. Coming to the course was a reaction to that.

It seems that the metaphors in the journeys caused Daniel to shift the focus of his narrative from his rash to his feelings of worthlessness and low self-esteem. This reinterpretation of his situation eliminated his need to understand the cause of the rash. His attitude towards his rash has changed – as he said, he saw the rash now as a wake-up call that drew his attention to the real issue that was preventing him from feeling self-fulfillment in his life.

In fact, the most profound and basic change Daniel recognised in his life as a result of the journeys had to do with his sense of self-worth and esteem:

> All I know is that since my work with the spirits, there has been a major, major shift in my life ... after the course I feel that I earn, and not just money-wise. I have more esteem and value for

myself. My time or my energy has worth. I do not allow myself to be taken for granted, both professionally and with friends.

Several explanations could account for Daniel's rapid physical healing following the course. One could be that simply believing he had received a real healing actually caused his rash to heal. This is related to what is known in medical language as the 'placebo effect' and we shall shortly address this issue fully.

Another explanation of the quick disappearance of Daniel's rash could be that the rash was related to issues of low self-esteem and the behavioural patterns that were pervading his life. Daniel's rash could then be explained as psychosomatic. We have already discussed the concept of psychosomatic illnesses in Chapter 5. From this perspective it could be argued that the fairy-tale metaphor had a profound effect on psychological factors, thus healing the physical symptoms (the rash) that accompanied them. According to Bettelheim,[15] not only does the fairy tale offer a solution to the problem, but it holds the promise for a 'happy' solution to be found. Although the metaphor or the story is comprehended by the intellect and cognitive domain, its main function is in the affective domain. It acts as a vehicle between the cognitive world and the affective world of feelings. Metaphors pervade our daily life, both in language, thought and action. We act and think in terms of our conceptual system – a system that is fundamentally metaphorical in nature.[16] The power of metaphors to influence our lives is thus grounded deep within our psyche. It never fails to amaze me how metaphors in journeys, in a gentle but pervasive way, direct and lead people to engage with their inner processes, connect with their inner power and, in this way, to be set free.

From a shamanic perspective, it would be argued that Daniel simply received a healing for his physical and psychological ailments from his spirit healers during the journeys. For the shaman, illness, whether physical or psychological, is explained in terms of power loss. From this perspective, the power animal for confidence would be considered to have restored some of the power which was lacking in Daniel. The teaching in the third journey, as well as the healings performed by the knight, the river and the elephant, were directed to empower him both psychologically and physically. The purpose of the shamanic healing is to create balance within the person, rather than to simply cure the disease. Daniel saw his physical healing to be part of the healing of his whole being.

THE MAGIC OF SHAMANIC JOURNEYS

We don't receive wisdom; we must discover it for ourselves after a journey that no one can take for us or spare us.

Marcel Proust

Now that we have explored the main mediums through which the spirits communicate with us during the shamanic journey, we finally reach the question – how does it work? How does the shamanic journey bring about transformation? In this section we explore different possible explanations, ranging from the psychological to the spiritual.

The effects of the shamanic journey have often been described by people as 'magical'. That may be for several reasons. For some, it is because shamanic work helped them heal from ailments or conditions which they were not able to cure using traditional therapies or medical interventions. For others, it is the speed by which the healing or transformations occurred. Both of these were clearly demonstrated in the case of Daniel.

Another example of the speed and effectiveness of shamanic work is a case of Marti, a Catalan child of 4 who was referred to me for shamanic work. Marti's school was complaining that the child was daydreaming, had no concentration, was not completing his tasks and was getting behind in comparison to other children. Although Marti was a loving and bright child, he was not communicating with his teachers or peer group very much. His mother went to see the school psychologist for advice and was instructed to use behaviour modification with the child. She was also told to have a notebook where his teacher would write daily feedback about Marti's behaviour and vice versa. Marti's mother was concerned about her child and a while later asked me if I could do some shamanic work to help Marti with his school situation.

I did a diagnostic journey for Marti and was instructed to do a soul retrieval and a power animal retrieval, with a month break in between. The main messages in my diagnostic journey indicated that the child simply needed some nurturing and one-to-one attention, especially from the mother. The instruction was for the mother to dedicate at least ten minutes during the day specifically and exclusively to the child. During that time Marti was to rest his head on her heart. This made sense to Marti's mother since, as she explained, he was only 2 when his brother was born. Marti's brother was extremely demanding, active and required a lot of his mother's attention. During the soul retrieval journey Marti was given a ritual to perform each morning for ten days. During that time he had to have a photograph of himself at the age of 1-year-old (the age of the soul I retrieved) by his bed. Each morning his mother was to show Marti the photograph and tell him how beautiful he looked at that age. Marti was then to hold the picture, kiss it and thank the soul for being with him.

Two days following the soul retrieval, the school wrote a letter to Marti's mother, informing her that Marti was completely transformed. He was focused in class, participating and completing assignments. A month later, Marti was still maintaining his performance in school. Not only that, but when returning from school and being asked how his day was, he started to answer, 'Very good,' instead of the silence that used to be his answer in the past. Since I do not speak Catalan, the child was sending feedbacks to me via his mother. Following the work he would send me weekly messages, telling me that he was sleeping well, being a good boy, that he was very happy, or simply handsome. What touched me about the feedback was that it was spontaneous and that Marti was actually noting for himself the changes that were happening to him.

Another reason that many people consider shamanic journeys to be magical is due to the fact that the healing and transformation which they experience after their journeys is lasting and that their problems don't come back. At times people don't even fully understand the messages or what happened on the journey at a conscious level, yet the change or healing still happens. This was also evident in the case of Daniel, who said that at the time he did the journeys and immediately afterwards, the messages he received did not make sense to him.

Other times, people actually receive on a shamanic journey information which they report they were already aware of, and yet, after the journey, the change which didn't happen for many years miraculously occurs.

Such a case was that of Rebecca, an Israeli woman in her fifties. Rebecca had an adult daughter who was diagnosed with light mental retardation. The entire family had been experiencing many difficulties in relation to the daughter's condition. These difficulties were expressed in feelings and behaviours of guilt, anger, rejection and denial. Rebecca, in particular, was more involved in the life of her daughter and was feeling extremely guilty about her child's condition. Her husband was in such denial regarding his daughter's condition that he even questioned whether the child was his. Her brothers were also rejecting her. With time, the child also developed compulsive behaviours, which confused and frightened her mother even more.

Rebecca was riddled with concerns regarding the future of her child. As she grew up and was becoming more and more independent, social services advised the family to place the young woman in a protected facility, so that she could gain a measure of independence in her life. Rebecca was not able to let go of her child and allow for that to happen. Throughout the years she had tried various therapeutic interventions, including channelling, in an attempt to heal her relationship with her daughter, but to no avail.

When she came to me she wished to address her relationship with her daughter. She went on a journey to receive a teaching on the subject. Immediately after returning from the journey, she told me that she was disappointed. Nothing the teachers told her was new to her. She said she already knew it all. A week later, however, I was surprised to receive a phone call from her, asking me for a second session. When we met she told me that she could not understand how, but somehow her attitude towards her daughter had changed. She said that some of the things that she knew before but could not put into practice were now starting to become easier for her to manage, following the journey.

Rebecca continued to work shamanically with the issue. Today, her daughter lives in a small group home, keeping regular contact with her family. The relationship between Rebecca's daughter and the rest of her family members is significantly improved. When asked in what way she thought the shamanic work had helped her in her relationship with her daughter, she replied:

> The shamanic journeys gradually brought me to the understanding that this was my daughter's path in life; that she will go wherever she needs to, with our help. I realised it was not for me to decide and determine what is right or wrong. I have come to terms with her path. This means, mainly, that she will not get married and that she will be alone. I am passed the fear of taking care of her like a 5-year-old child. The doubts, the fears, the uncertainties, all went away. I didn't need to be in control of her path any more. In the past I had carried anger for a long time. Now when I am angry with her, it passes quickly and I am able to hug and kiss her immediately. I accept her behaviours much easier. I explode very little now. I am not afraid any more that something bad will happen to her. In the past I was speaking for her; now I am able to let her speak for herself. I received similar messages to those of my shamanic journeys in a channelling once, but I didn't

understand them. The channelling scared me. The shamanic journey made the connections for me and I was able to put the messages into practice. It wasn't frightening or threatening. I was going on the journey and experiencing it and it was a process, there was preparation, formulating the mission, writing it, talking it. It was going through a process and that was fun.

What is magic?

The stories of Daniel, Marti and Rebecca are just three examples of the 'magical' effectiveness of the shamanic journey. Throughout this book I have presented the stories of many others. The question remains, however, what do we mean by 'magical'? What is magic?

In one of my shamanic journeys I received a message about magic, which stayed with me. When I asked my teacher what magic was, he told me, 'Strike a match and it lights. What is that? To a child that does not know anything about the chemistry and the process that it went through to be created, it's magic. To a person who has never been in a lift, what happens in there is magic. Press a button and the box moves.'

When I first received the message I was not satisfied. I still felt that my question had not been answered. After returning from the journey I contemplated my teacher's words and a deeper meaning became apparent to me. We often refer to things as magical when they are either unexpected, surprising or happen effortlessly. Put simply, we refer to things as magical when we can't explain them or when we don't understand them. Thus, when something does not behave in a manner in which we expect it to behave, according to our rules of how the world is, we may perceive it as 'magic'.

Since we have stripped our world of its spirit dimension, since for modern people the idea of a spirit world which exists parallel to ours is less than acceptable, so the shamanic journey, which is based in that invisible reality, may hold elements of magic for us. For the person in the Amazons, the works of the shaman are not magic, simply medicine. While we regard our own doctors to be scientists rather than magicians, the injection that a western doctor gives to a South American tribesman may be perceived as magic by them. That does not mean that either the tribesman or the westerner is ignorant. It simply means that the two hold different ways of understanding and conceptualising the world.

What often happens, however, when two worldviews clash, is that one attempts to explain the other using its own rules and conceptions. Western psychologists and anthropologists, for example, may ignore or dismiss the shaman's spirit-based explanation as to the workings of shamanic healing, attempting to force a western logic upon it. This may be equally true in the case of the tribesman, who may attribute the healing powers of the doctor's injection to the spirit which resides within it.

JOURNEY AS A VEHICLE FOR TRANSFORMATION

Many different explanations could account for the magical effects that shamanic journeys have had on people's lives, ranging from the psychological to the spiritual. Let us explore a few of them.

Relaxation and self-hypnosis

Shamanic journeys involve entering into an ASC. Certain forms of ASC are known to facilitate psychological as well as physical well-being. One of the most well-known of these states is relaxation. The state of relaxation can, on its own, relieve both psychological and physical stress-based ailments. Hence, some would claim that while journeying shamanically one is also entering into a deep state of relaxation, and that it is due to that fact that certain stress-related conditions are healed following the journey. This is, however, a problematic argument, since shamanic intervention is known to heal more than just stress-related conditions. Furthermore, it is clear that this explanation cannot account for the instances in which the person who is healed is not journeying themselves, as is the case with soul retrievals, for example.

Entering a shamanic state of consciousness is also regarded by some to be a form of self-hypnosis. Numerous studies indicate that self-hypnosis may be most effective in facilitating change. When people go under hypnosis they receive messages on a subliminal level of consciousness. It is believed that receiving the messages while in this form of ASC is what facilitates the desired shift in behaviour. If one considers the shamanic journey to be a form of self-hypnosis, then its effectiveness can be attributed to the suggestions one has received from the spirits during the journey. Although, unlike the relaxation theory, this explanation could account for more of the changes we observe in people following shamanic journeys, I believe it still cannot account for all of them.

The placebo effect

Another popular explanation to the effectiveness of shamanic journeys refers to the placebo effect. The actual word 'placebo' is derived from Latin, meaning 'I shall please'. A placebo can be any pill, medicine or surgical intervention which has no active medicinal components in it. For example, a sugar pill or a saline injection is a placebo. The word is well known in the medical world to refer to cases in which people respond to a placebo as if it had active chemical components in it. For example, when receiving an injection of saline and being told that they are receiving an injection of morphine, many people experience dramatic pain relief.

Numerous studies have been conducted to explore what has come to be known as the 'placebo effect'. Clearly, a sugar pill does not bring about physical healing. In cases where it has, the agent which is credited for creating the change on a physical level is our own mind. The human mind is acknowledged to have such a potent effect on the body, that when conducting medical studies the placebo effect is always controlled for. Clear-cut evidence has been found regarding the potency of the placebo effect in managing pain. However, its effects are not limited to pain relief. The placebo effect is regarded to facilitate healing in up to 70 per cent of all medical and surgical interventions.[17]

The potency of the placebo effect can go either way. Cannon[18] researched the effects of black magic and sorcery and reached interesting conclusions. He claimed that certain magical practices are of great potency, to the degree that a person cursed to death by a sorcerer would actually die as a result. However, he also claimed that for the magic to be effective, both the person, the sorcerer and the community to which they belonged must hold a strong belief in the effectiveness of the magical act. It has been demonstrated that fear is associated with extremely intense activity of the sympathetic nervous system, which could result in eventual death. The opposite, however, is also true. It was demonstrated that people who held a genuinely deep belief that they had recovered from a terminal illness actually did recover, against all medical odds.[19] The important point for our discussion here is the evidence which points to the power of our mind to create changes on a physiological level.

The placebo effect is also used by many in an attempt to explain how the shamanic journey works. The basic claim here is that due to a person's belief or expectation of receiving a healing, they actually are healed. Thus, the experiences and the messages which we receive during the journey coupled with the fact that we receive them while being in a deep ASC, may affect our well-being through the workings of our own mind.

The creative power of thoughts

To acknowledge the power of the placebo effect is to acknowledge the fact that our thought has the power to create change in our physical body. It is a well-established fact that all thoughts produce chemical reactions in our brain and body. We still know relatively little about the actual mechanics of this process, but what we do know for sure is that thought is creative. It is not only evidence from the medical or therapeutic fields which points to this fact, or the numerous teachings of mystic and spiritual practices, but also relatively recent research conducted by quantum physicists. This research has yielded surprising evidence which points to the fact that our thoughts not only affect our own body, but also our environment and reality.

The film *What the BLEEP do we know!?* brought the notion that thought is creative more into the open by reviewing the different theories and interviewing scientists and thinkers of different fields on the subject. One of the examples presented in the film is the fascinating experiment conducted by Dr Masaru Emoto of Japan. Dr Emoto examined the molecular structure of water and attempted to affect it using mental stimuli alone. In a series of studies he taped labels on several identical water containers and then photographed the water molecules using a special microscope. The results of the study were stunning. The shape of the water molecules differed considerably from container to container. For example, the shape of a molecule within a container labelled 'thank you' looked nothing like a molecule within a container labelled 'I hate you'. Emoto concluded that it was the human thought or intent which was the driving force behind the structural change of the molecules.

Unfortunately, most people are not aware of the power of their thoughts, and the degree to which their thoughts affect their lives. This brings us back to our earlier discussion about magic. There is yet another way to look at magic. A woman in Israel journeyed to ask for a teaching about magic. On her journey she met Houdini, who told her:

> *Magic is transformation. The existence of the universe is the movement of the atoms. Transformation happens when you apply human thought to this movement. So any transformation, any change, is magic. Existence is full of magic. You simply don't give it its place. You do*

not honour it. This is what I have learnt; I have learnt to respect magic and that is why I could stretch the boundaries of the ordinary reality into the non-ordinary reality and create magic. What does abracadabra mean? It is just a word, letters that have no content. It is the meaning and intention that is put into this word that creates the magic. Magic is the transformation of content; it is the transformation of contents and meanings into purposes and aims. You must first determine what your purpose is. The instrument can be a word, a letter, a specific situation, a specific substance that you wish to imbue with different meanings and contents. By defining the purpose and with the help of willpower, thought and imagination you can create magic. Every creation is magic. You have a piece of paper and colours and each one of them on its own has no power, but when you draw a picture, magic happens. And if you want to give the picture meaning, content and purpose, you can draw the Mona Lisa.

The explanation given by my own spirit teachers echoes the teachings of this journey as well:

When you let go of fears, inhibitions, limiting belief systems, then you can have what you want. That is magic. The inventor thinks of magical things happening, the impossible, then creates it. You are all creators of magic. Magic is part of your daily life. You want a more scientific explanation. My explanations are too simple for you. Because you see magic as non-ordinary, as extraordinary.

Drawing on the teachings of the spirits and the findings regarding the potency of the placebo effect could help us to realise that we are the creators of our own magic, our own reality. In this sense the shamanic journey could be seen as a vehicle for transformation, which may help us to alter our own limiting beliefs and connect us with our inner power. It is when we truly come in touch with that power within us that we are able to create magic in our daily lives.

Transcending the boundaries of the ego

There is yet another explanation of the workings of the shamanic journey. Beyond all of the psychological or therapeutic mechanisms which might be involved in the process of shamanic healing, lies also a spiritual one. I believe that the power of shamanic healing lies to a great extent in the fact that the shamanic journey connects us with power and wisdom. What happens when we hear the drums and go into an ASC is literally that our consciousness is transformed. We don't process anything from the same perspective that we do while in an ordinary state of consciousness. Rather, we experience a state of existence which lies beyond our ego boundaries. By ego I am referring to our past conditioning and belief systems, our fears, our self-saboteurs, our rational thinking, our very personality.

While journeying, the teachers we meet are always experienced as external to our mind. Whether we would consider these teachers to be figments of our imagination, a manifestation of the Jungian archetypes, or actual existing spirits, the messages which we receive from them are not limited by our mind and its self-generating monologues. While journeying, we become receptive to wisdom and healing which far surpass that which is found within our own ego-boundaries.

We venture into a reality that is not controlled by our limitations and thus we experience a fragment of the true nature of the universe. We experience truth. Our mind is no longer coloured by fears and doubts, and by our limiting belief system. The shamanic journey connects us with power because it connects us with truth. It is a truth that we already know, deep within us; a truth which is usually hidden from us, buried under the layers of our ego.

Beyond psychology

Up until now we have explored different explanations which could account for the power of the shamanic journey to heal. It may very well be true that each of the suggested mechanisms play a part in the process of shamanic healing. However, evidence exists which cannot be explained by any of them.

Evidence, or rather, reports, of parapsychological displays by shamans are very common. Many anthropologists have reported shamans performing healings and divinations which cannot be scientifically explained. One of the most impressive and well documented cases is that of Don José, the Huichol shaman who performed a rainmaking ceremony in California after the region had been suffering from a prolonged drought. The ceremony was filmed by a television crew, who also filmed, the next day, the rain pouring from the skies.

Victor Blanco, in his book *The Blue Deer*[20] tells of a time when he participated in a shamanic ritual during which he saw a beautiful woman rising from the fire and inviting him to come with her, telling him that she was death. After returning from his trance state, he was shocked to find out that the rest of his companions had sensed the presence of Mukiyara, the death goddess and were fighting for his life while he was conversing with her. Such experiences of 'collective hallucination' are extremely common, yet unexplainable by any psychological or scientific means.

Many testimonies of miraculous, unexplainable healings performed by shamans around the world are also documented. One such example is that of Doña Pachita, a legendary healer and shaman from Mexico. Using a simple knife, the Mexican healer was observed closely by western anthropologists, medical doctors and others (who at times even participated themselves in the procedures). Pachita performed surgery without the use of anaesthetics, with remarkable positive results. Evidence exists of people recovering completely from cancer and other severe illnesses following a single operation by this woman. Her healings are well documented in the works of Dr J Grinberg-Zilberbaum.[21]

However, it is not only among shamanic cultures that we come across what seems to be evidence for the existence of a spirit world. It is also in my own work with people, throughout the years, that I have come across many cases which could not be explained by any of the theoretical suggestions made up until now. This is most evident when working with children. One such case was the case of Marti, the 4-year-old whose story I presented earlier in this chapter. Another example was presented in Chapter 5 in the case of Yarin, who was seeing insects in his food. Yet another example is that of Benjamin.

Five-year-old Benjamin, youngest of three children, had been struggling with an intermittent stammer for some considerable time. This was recognised by both parents and teaching staff, leading to a referral for speech therapy. It was during the initial assessment that it became clear that the root cause of his condition was psychological and not physical. Therefore, the speech therapist decided that her intervention would not be of benefit to the child. Benjamin also exhibited introverted behaviour. He behaved older than his years, and was experiencing difficulties interacting and playing with his peers. He had been referred to a psychologist who worked with him for some considerable time with little or no improvement in his speech pattern or behaviour. Benjamin was no longer in therapy when he was referred to me for shamanic work.

Benjamin's parents were separated before he was born. The children lived with the mother, but had regular contact with the father. Benjamin's mother observed that his stammering worsened following these visits. She thought the reason for this was because he did not want to visit his father. The relationship between the parents was very acrimonious and some of this acrimony was demonstrated in the presence of the children.

Normally in cases like this, I would have embarked upon a diagnostic journey to ask my spirit teachers for guidance and help. However, it was apparent to me that there was a great deal of pressure on the child, both from the parents and the school, regarding his speech impediment. I decided, based on my experience of working with children and my experience as a shamanic counsellor, to perform a power animal retrieval to give Benjamin the strength and support he needed to cope with the pressure he was under at that time.

The power animal journey I made addressed several issues. The direct teaching from my guardian spirit clearly indicated that the acrimony between the parents was impacting strongly on the children and that their style of communication with each other was affecting Benjamin's presenting problem in particular. Further explanation given to me regarding this child was that he was afraid, lacked confidence, felt himself powerless and lost. I was further instructed to do another journey for the child to retrieve a lost soul.

I retrieved the soul of a newborn baby. My teacher stated that the baby soul would complete the child, calm him and give him confidence. When Benjamin's mother first came to see me, she kept saying that she felt there was something missing in her son, and that he was incomplete. Following the journey, she explained that during her pregnancy she had experienced a great deal of sadness and anger as a result of the death of her father, and that her marriage was on the verge of breaking down. She was not surprised, therefore, that the soul was that of a newborn baby.

Following the two journeys the change in Benjamin was almost instantaneous. His stammering stopped, he became more open and communicative with those around him, and he began to develop friendships with other children. He actually approached his mother the day after his soul retrieval and told her, 'Who was mummy's sad little boy yesterday, and is happy today?' His mother said that after the soul retrieval, she had a sense that the child was more complete, as if something had been returned to him and made him whole. She also noticed other significant behavioural changes in him. She said that while before the journey Benjamin had been very a quiet and obedient child, he was now more happy and outgoing and was beginning to stand up for his own rights and even argue to make his point.

In this chapter we have attempted to understand the magic of shamanic journeys. This has not been an easy task. I believe that the reason for that is simply because we are looking at a phenomenon which stems from one worldview and attempting to understand it using another. The explanation given by shamans as to the workings and effectiveness of the shamanic journey would obviously differ considerably from those we have suggested above. Since the shaman considers illness to originate from a loss of power or soul to begin with, the healings we have presented here would equally and simply be explained by a shaman to be a result of that power or soul having been restored. Once this equilibrium of the soul has been gained, health is merely the natural course of events.

The cases of Yarin, Marti or Benjamin could not be explained by any of the theoretical explanations given earlier. None of them actually experienced shamanic journeying themselves. In two of the cases the children were very young and none of them even spoke my language. Although simple explanations were given to the children as to the process of shamanic healing, none of them asked many questions or attempted to analyse or understand the messages given by my spirit teachers during the journeys. Not only that, but the shamanic work was extremely short term and carried significant results, which were not achieved using traditional western therapies.

I find that confronted with evidence of this sort, the shaman's explanation may be the most plausible one. Perhaps in order to truly understand and be able to enter the world of the shaman, we must attempt to adopt the shamanic worldview, rather than force our own upon it. As anthropologist Edith Turner demonstrates, we might actually have much to gain by fully and totally allowing ourselves to be immersed in the wondrous world of the shaman:

> To my surprise, the healing of the second patient culminated in my sighting a spirit form . . . The traditional doctor bent down amid the singing and drumming to extract the harmful spirit . . . I saw with my own eyes a large gray blob of something like plasma emerge from the sick woman's back. Then I knew the Africans were right. There is spirit stuff, there is spirit affliction: it isn't a matter of metaphor and symbol, or even psychology. And I began to see how anthropologists have perpetuated an endless series of put-downs about the many spirit events in which they participate – 'participated' in a kindly pretence. They might have obtained valuable material, but they have been operating with the wrong paradigm, that of the positivists' denial. To reach a peak experience in a ritual, it really is necessary to sink oneself fully in it. Thus for me, 'going native' achieved a breakthrough to an altogether different worldview, foreign to academia, by means of which certain material was chronicled that could have been gathered in no other way.[21]

THE DISENCHANTMENT OF THE WORLD

In his paper, 'Science as a Vocation', Max Weber[23] writes: 'The fate of our times is characterized by rationalization and intellectualization and, above all, by the "disenchantment of the world".' He claims that through the rationalisation and intellectualisation created by science, the world of modern man has been stripped of magic and mystery; it has become disenchanted.

This disenchantment does not imply that we know our world better or understand in full the conditions under which we live. Weber claims that as modern people we do not understand our world better than does the African tribesman. But rather we have the knowledge or belief that we could gain an understanding of it, if only we wished. This in effect strips our world of its magic, making every element of existence calculable and discernable. That is the disenchantment of the world: 'One need no longer have recourse to magical means in order to master or implore the spirits, as did the savage, for whom such mysterious powers existed. Technical means and calculations perform the service. This above all is what intellectualization means.'[24]

With science, rationality and materialism, we have stripped the world of magic and mystery. So many of us have come to believe that reality is only that which we can observe through known scientific means. We are left with a world that is all observable and can be dissected at will; all that is unknown and mysterious has been removed. But this knowing or understanding has also opened a hole in our lives. Somehow, alongside mystery, meaning has also been lost. The keys to knowledge offered to us by science are also the keys that have locked us up in the cage of our own rationality. We have lost our connection with nature, with mystery, with all of creation itself. But the craving for magic is still within us.

It is this longing, I believe, which is bringing shamanism, humanity's most ancient spiritual and healing tradition, back into our lives. It is our spiritual heritage, and the more we practise it, the more we remember and regain that which we have lost. For tens of thousands of years shamanic practices supported our ancestors. I believe shamanism still has much to offer us today. It has survived centuries of change to return to us, bearing not only healing, but the magic and mystery we have craved for. As with everything in our lives, we have tried and are trying to understand the magic that is shamanism, but perhaps this attempt is a futile one. I believe we may be wiser to relinquish it altogether and simply allow it to be.

References

Introduction

1. Gallegos, E.S. (1985) *The Personal Totem Pole*. Santa Fe, NM: Moon Bear Press. Gallegos, E.S. (1991) *Animals of the Four Windows*. Santa Fe, NM: Moon Bear Press. Gallegos, E.S. (1993) *Little Ed & Golden Bear*. Santa Fe, NM: Moon Bear Press.

Chapter 1 Shamanism: Basic Definitions

1. Eliade, M. (1964) Shamanism: *Archaic Techniques of Ecstasy*. London: Penguin Arkana.
2. New Scientist (1996) *Passions run high over French cave art*, 4 May: 8.
3. 3 Eliade, M. (1964).
4. 4 *Ibid.*, pp. 3–5.
5. 5 Lewis, I.M. (1971) *Ecstatic Religion: A Study of Shamanism and Spirit Possession*. London: Penguin.
6. Dioszegi, V. (1968) *Tracing Shamans in Siberia*. Oosterhout, the Netherlands: Anthropological Publications.
7. Halifax, J. (1979) *Shamanic Voices: A Survey of Visionary Narratives,* p. 3. New York: Penguin Arkana.
8. Hutton, R. (2001) *Shamans: Siberian Spirituality and the Western Imagination,* p. 47. London: Hambledon and London.
9. Eliade, M. (1964).
10. *Ibid.*, p.20.
11. *Ibid.*, p. 5.
12. Harner, M.J. (1980) *The Way of the Shaman: A Guide to Power and Healing*, p. 20. San Francisco: Harper & Row.
13. *Ibid.*
14. Harner, M. (1987) *The ancient wisdom in shamanic cultures*, in S. Nicholson (ed.) *Shamanism*, pp. 3–16. Wheaton, IL: Quest.
15. Eliade, M. and Couliano, I.P. (2000) *The HarperCollins Concise Guide to World Religions,* p. 214. San Francisco: Harper.
16. Harner, M.J. (1980), p. xii.
17. Eliade, M. (1964).
18. Shirokogoroff, S.M. ([1935 first edition] 1982) *Psychomental Complex of the Tungus*. London: Kegan Paul, Trench, Trubner.
19. Lewis, I.M. (1981), *What is a Shaman?* Folk, Dansk Etnografisk Tidsskrift, 23.
20. Hutton, R. (2001).
21. Jacobsen, M.D. (1999) *Shamanism: Traditional and Contemporary Approaches to the Mastery of Spirits and Healing*, p. 9. New York: Berghahn Books.

22 Eliade, M. (1964).
23 Winkelman, M.J. (1992) *Shamans, Priests and Witches: A Cross Cultural Study of Magico-Religious Practitioners*. Anthropological Research Paper of Arizona State University. Tempa, AZ: Arizona University Press.
24 Castaneda, C. (1968) *The Teachings of Don Juan: A Yaqui Way of Knowledge*. Berkeley, CA: University of California Press.
25 Harner, M.J. (1980).
26 Wagley, C. (1977) *Welcome of Tears: The Tapirape Indians of Central Brazil*, p. 184. Prospect Heights, IL: Waveland Press.
27 Karseten, R. (1935) *The head-hunters of Western Amazonas: the life and culture of the Jibaro Indians of Eastern Ecuador and Peru. Societas Scientiarum Fennica, Commentationes Humanarum Litterarum*, 7(1): 444–445.
28 Bogoras, W. (1908) *The Chukchee*, p. 281. Leiden: Brill.

Chapter 2 The Shaman's Dream: Calling and Initiation

1 Hutton, R. (2001) *Shamans: Siberian Spirituality and the Western Imagination*. London: Hambledon and London.
2 Kaplan, J.O. (1975) *The Piaroa: A People of the Orinoco Basin*. Oxford: Clarendon Press.
3 Megged, N. (1998) *Portals of Hope and Gates of Terror: Shamanism, Magic and Witchcraft in South and Central America*, p. 407. Tel Aviv: Modan Press.
4 Handelman, D. (1967) *The development of a Washo shaman*, Ethnology, 6: 444–464.
5 Wagley, C. (1977) *Welcome of Tears: The Tapirape Indians of Central Brazil*, p. 198. Prospect Heights, IL: Waveland Press.
6 Rasmussen, K. (1930) *Intellectual Culture of the Hudson Bay Eskimos*. Report of the Fifth Thule Expedition, 1921–1924, Vol. 7, part I, pp. 52–5. Copenhagen: Gyldendal.
6 Wagley, C. (1977).
7 8 Hutton, R. (2001) p. 70.
8 9 Bogoras, W. (1908) *The Chukcheep*, p. 53. Leiden: Brill.
10 Devereux, G. (1956) *Normal and abnormal: the key problem of psychiatric anthropology, in Some Uses of Anthropology: Theoretical and Applied*. Washington: The Anthropological Society of Washington.
11 *Ibid*.
12 Eliade, M. (1964) *Shamanism: Archaic Techniques of Ecstasy*. London: Penguin Arkana.
13 *Ibid*.
14 *Ibid*., p. 86.
15 Eliade, M. (1964).
16 *Ibid*., pp. 39–42.

17 Harner, M.J. (1972) *The Jivaro: People of the Sacred Waterfalls.* Garden City: Double-day/Natural History Press.
18 Walsh, R. (1990) *The Spirit of Shamanism,* p. 59. London: Mandala.
19 Walsh, R. (1990), p. 69.
20 Noll, R. (1983) *Shamanism and schizophrenia: a state-specific approach to the 'schizophrenia metaphor' of shamanic states,* American Ethnologist, 10(3): 443– 459.
21 Achterberg, J. (1985) *Imagery and Healing: Shamanism and Modern Medicine,* p. 30. Boston, MA: New Science Library.
22 Noll, R. (1983), pp.443–59.
23 Wilber, K. (1980) *The Atman Project.* Wheaton, IL:Quest.
24 Hillman, J. (1975) *Re-Visioning Psychology.* New York: Harper & Row.
25 Noll, R. (1983).
26 Eliade, M. (1964), p. 29.
27 Walsh, R. (1990), p. 91.
28 Perry, J. (1986) *Spiritual emergency and renewal,* Revision, 8(2): 33-40
29 Halifax, J. (1979) *Shamanic Voices: A Survey of Visionary Narratives,* p.11. New York: Penguin Arkana
30 Hutton, R. (2001), p.72.
31 Popov, A. (1968) *How Sereptie Djarvoskin of the Nganasans (Tavgi Samoyeds) became a shaman,* in V. Diószegi (ed.) *Popular Beliefs and Folklore Tradition in Siberia,* pp. 137–146. Bloomington, IN: Indiana University Press.
32 Eliade, M. (1964), p. 39.
33 Achterberg, J. (1985), p. 118.
34 Eliade, M. (1964), p. 83.
35 Narby, J. and Huxley, F. (2001) *Shamans Through Time: 500 Years on the Path to Knowledge,* p. 53. New York: Jeremy P. Tarcher/Putnam.
36 Hutton, R. (2001), pp. 70–1.
37 Wagley, C. (1977), p. 199.

Chapter 3 Gateway to the Spirits: Shamanic Worlds, Shamanic Journeys

1 Eliade, M. (1964) *Shamanism: Archaic Techniques of Ecstasy,* p. 259. London: Penguin Arkana.
2 Halifax, J. (1979) *Shamanic Voices: A Survey of Visionary Narratives,* p. 1. New York: Penguin Arkana.
3 Peters, L.G. and Price-Williams, D. (1980) *Towards an experiential analysis of shamanism,* American Ethnologist, 7: 398–418.
4 Walsh, R. (1990) *The Spirit of Shamanism.* London: Mandala.
5 Tart, C. (1983) *States of Consciousness.* El Cerrito, CA: Psychological Processes.

6　Wasson, R.G. (1968) *Divine Mushroom of Immortality*. New York: Harcourt Brace, Jovanovich. Harner, M.J. (1973) *Hallucinogens and Shamanism*. New York: Oxford University Press. Stafford, P. (1983) *Psychedelics Encyclopaedia*, revised edn. Los Angeles: Tarcher.

7　Tart, C. (1983).

8　Neher, A. (1961) *Auditory driving observed with scalp electrodes in normal subjects*, EEG and Clinical Neurophysiology, 13: 449–451.

9　Popov, A. (1968) H*ow Sereptie Djarvoskin of the Nganasans* (Tavgi Samoyeds) *became a shaman,* in V. Diószegi (ed.) *Popular Beliefs and Folklore Tradition in Siberia*, pp. 137–46. Bloomington, IN: Indiana University Press.

10　Handelman, D. (1967) *The development of a Washo shaman*, Ethnology, 6: 444–64.

11　Krippner, S. and Villodo, A. (1976) *The Realms of Healing*. Milbrae, CA: Celestial Arts.

12　Megged, N. (1998) *Portals of Hope and Gates of Terror: Shamanism, Magic and Witchcraft in South and Central America*. Tel Aviv: Modan Press.

13　Ibid.

14　Harner, M.J. (1988) *Helping reawaken shamanism among the Sami (Laplanders) of northernmost Europe*, The Foundation for Shamanic Studies Newsletter, 1(3).

15　Harner, M.J. (1980) *The Way of the Shaman: A Guide to Power and Healing*. San Francisco: Harper & Row.

16　Eliade, M. (1964), p. 315.

17　Frank, J. (1985) *Therapeutic components shared by all psychotherapies*, in M. Mahoney and A. Freeman (eds) *Cognition and Psychotherapy*, p. 49. New York: Plenum.

18　Mussen, P.H. (ed.) (1983) *Piaget's theory, in Handbook of Child Psychology*, Vol. 1. New York: Wiley.

19　Eliade, M. (1964), p. 39.

Chapter 4 Beyond the Ego: Spirits and Spirituality

1　Campbell, J. (1983) *The Way of the Animal Powers*, Vol. 1, p. 169. San Francisco: Harper & Row.

2　Jung, C.G. (1959) *The Archetypes and the Collective Unconscious*. Princeton, NJ: Princeton University Press.

3　Gurdjieff, G. I. (1973) *Views From the Real World*. New York: E.P. Dutton.

4　Jung, C.G. (1959).

5　Castaneda, C. (1968) *The Teachings of Don Juan: A Yaqui Way of Knowledge*. Berkeley, CA: University of California Press.

6　Walsh, R. (1990) *The Spirit of Shamanism*, p. 137. London: Mandala.

7　Jeffers, S. (1991) *Feel the Fear and Do It Anyway*. London: Arrow Books.

8　Sisson, C.P. (1996) *Inner Adventures*, p. 22. Auckland, NZ: Total Press.

Chapter 5 The Ancient and the Modern: Shamanic Healing

1. Kleinman, A. and Sung, L.H. (1979) *Why do indigenous practitioners successfully heal?* Social Sciences and Medicine, 13B: 7–26.
2. Achterberg, J. (1988) *The wounded healer: transformational journeys in modern medicine,* in G. Door (ed.) *Shaman's Path: Healing, Personal Growth, & Empowerment,* pp. 115–126. Boston, MA: Shambhala.
3. Bates, B. (1996) *The Way of the Wyrd: Teachings for Today from Our Ancient Past.* London: Rider.
4. Rogers, S. (1942) *Shamans and medicine men,* CIBA Symposia, 4: 1202–1223.
5. Basilov, V.N. (1984) *Chosen by the spirits,* in M. Balzer (ed.) *Shamanism,* pp. 1–46. Moscow: Politizdat.
6. Helman, C.G. (1994) *Doctor-patient relations,* in *Culture Health and Illness.* London: Butterworth Heinemann.
7. Kleinman, A. and Sung, L.H. (1979).
8. Benedict, E. and Porter, T. (1977) *Native Indian medicine ways,* Monchanin Journal, 10: 11–22.
9. Lipowski, Z.J. (1977) *Psychosomatic medicine in the seventies: an overview,* The American Journal of Psychiatry, 134(3): 233–238.
10. Pelletier, K. (1977) *Mind as Healer, Mind as Slayer.* New York: Dell.
11. Achterberg, J. (1985) *Imagery and Healing: Shamanism and Modern Medicine,* p. 146. Boston, MA: New Science Library.
12. Bates, B. (1996).
13. Achterberg, J. (1985), pp. 19–20.
14. Eliade, M. (1964) *Shamanism: Archaic Techniques of Ecstasy.* London: Penguin Arkana.
15. Megged, N. (1998) *Portals of Hope and Gates of Terror: Shamanism, Magic and Witchcraft in South and Central America,* p. 93. Tel Aviv: Modan Press.
16. Harner, M.J. (1972) *The Jivaro: People of the Sacred Waterfalls.* Garden City: Double-day/Natural History Press.
17. Eliade, M. (1964).
18. Ingerman, S. (1991) *Soul Retrieval: Mending the Fragmented Self.* San Francisco: Harper.
19. Jung, C.G. (1959) *The Archetypes and the Collective Unconscious.* Princeton, NJ: Princeton University Press.
20. Eliade, M. (1964), p. 217.
21. Eliade, M. (1964), p. 220.
22. Henry, A. (1903) *The Lolos and Other Tribes of Western China,* JRAI, 33: 96–107. Marshall, H.I. (1922) *The Karen People of Burma: A Study in Anthropology and Ethnology.* Columbus, OH: State University Press.
23. Harner, M.J. (1980) *The Way of the Shaman: A Guide to Power and Healing,* pp. 69–70. San Francisco: Harper & Row.

24 Horwitz, J. (1995) *Animism: everyday magic, Sacred Hoop*, 9: 6–10.
25 Megged, N. (1998) *Portals of Hope and Gates of Terror: Shamanism, Magic and Witchcraft in South and Central America*, pp. 67–8. Tel Aviv: Modan Press.
26 Megged, N. (1998), p. 75.
27 Hopkins, J. (1984) *The Tantric Distinction: An Introduction to Tibetan Buddhism.* London: Wisdom.
28 Rasmussen, K. (1927) *Intellectual Culture of the Iglulik Eskimos.* Copenhagen: Gyldendalske Boghandel, Nordisk Forlag.
29 Smith, C.M. (1997) *Jung and Shamanism in Dialogue*, p. 139. New Jersey: Paulist Press.
30 Megged, N. (1998).
31 Horwitz, J. (2002) *Power in your hand: a short introduction to the rattle, Sacred Hoop*, 36.
32 Harner, M.J. (1980).

Chapter 6 The Magic of Shamanism: the Journey as a Vehicle for Transformation

1 Noll, R. (1985) *Mental imagery cultivation as a cultural phenomenon: the role of visions in shamanism*, Current Anthropology, 26(4): 443–451.
2 Achterberg, J. (1985) *Imagery and Healing: Shamanism and Modern Medicine.* Boston, MA: New Science Library.
3 Achterberg, J. (1988) *The wounded healer: transformational journeys in modern medicine*, in G. Door (ed.), *Shaman's Path: Healing, Personal Growth, & Empowerment*, p. 115. Boston, MA: Shambhala.
4 Smith, C.M. (1997) *Jung and Shamanism in Dialogue.* New Jersey: Paulist Press.
5 Turbayne, C.M. (1970) *The Myth of Metaphor.* Columbia, SC: University of South Carolina Press.
6 Gold, J. (1990) *Read for Your Life: Literature as a Life Support System.* Markham, Ontario: Fitzhenry & Whiteside.
7 Ornstein, R. (1972) *The Psychology of Consciousness.* New York: Viking.
8 Watzlawick, P. (1978) *The Language of Chang*, pp. 14–15. New York: Basic Books.
9 McMullen, L. (1989) *Use of Figurative Language in Successful and Unsuccessful Case of Psychotherapy: Three Comparisons.* Metaphor and Symbolic Activity, 4: 203–225.
10 Grinder J. and Bandler, R. (1976) *The Structure of Magic*, Vol. 2. Palo Alto, CA: Science and Behaviour. Grinder J. and Bandler, R. (1981) *Trance-formations: Neuro-linguistic Programming and the Structure of Hypnotic Experience.* Moab, UT: Real People Press.
11 Bettelheim, B. (1977). *The Uses of Enchantment.* New York: Vintage.
12 Ibid.

13 Cameron-Bandler, L. (1978) *They Lived Happily Ever After: A Book About Achieving Happy Endings in Coupling.* Cupertino, CA: Meta Publications.

14 Gadamar, H.G. (1960) *Wahrheit und Methode.* Tübingen: Mohr.

15 Bettelheim, B. (1977).

16 Lakoff, G. and Johnson, M. (1980) *Metaphors We Live By.* Chicago: University of Chicago Press.

17 Wolf, S. (1950) *Effects of suggestion and conditioning on the action of chemical agents in human subjects: the pharmacology of placebos,* Journal of Clinical Investigation, 29: 100–109.

18 Cannon, W.B. (1957) *Voodoo death, Psychosomatic Medicine*, 19: 182–190.

19 Achterberg, J. (1985).

20 Blanco, V. (1991) *The Blue Deer.* Mexico: Diana.

21 Grinberg-Zilberbaum, J. (1998) *Las Manifestaciones del Ser I, II.* Edamex, Mexico.

22 Turner, E. (2003) *The reality of spirits*, in G. Harvey (ed.) *Shamanism: A Reade*, p. 145. London: Routledge.

23 Weber, M. (1948) *Science as a vocation,* in *Essays in Sociology*, pp. 129–156.

24 *Ibid.*

Index

Abraham, spirit teacher 117
Achterberg, Jeanne 42, 144, 191
active imagination 194
   see also imagery work
alcohol 15
Altamira cave, Spain 4
altered states of consciousness *see* ASC
Anglo-Saxons 139
animal double 71, 150
animal kingdom 167-170
animal spirits 71-72
animals of power *see* power animals,
animism 13, 17
   communication and 50, 184-187
apprenticeship training 43-46
archetypes 10, 113, 121, 229
art therapy 193
Arunta people 63
ASC (altered state(s) of consciousness)
access to wisdom through 49, 120, 229-230
   for communication with spirits 14, 183
   maintenance of 60
   metaphors received in 202
   mysticism and 51
   shamanic control of consciousness 12, 33, 196-197
   shamanic journey through *see* shamanic journeys
   shamans as masters of ecstasy 6, 33
   stages of induction of 49
   techniques for inducing 55-61
   therapeutic effects of 224
   the uniqueness of the shamanic state (SSC) 51-52
   western psychology and 34
auditory stimulation 59-61
Avvakum Petrov 4
axis mundi 13, 50, 74
ayahuasca 57

Bahanarotu shaman 74, 76
Bai Ulgen 49
Bates, Brian 144
bereavement 101-104

Bettelheim, B. 211, 216
Biet, Antoin 45
Biofeedback 193
Blanco, Victor 230
body movements 59
Bogoras, W. 26
brain processes 200
brainwaves 61
Buddhism 56, 86
deity yoga 171

call, shamanic 21-28
   denying the call 26
   initiatory call and experiences 27-32 *see also* initiation crises
Castaneda, Carlos 15, 121
   see also Don Juan
cave paintings 4, 168
chanting 59
Chauvet cave, France 4
Chukchi tribe 16, 21, 26
collective hallucination 230
collective unconscious 121
community 142
Conibo Indians 63
consciousness
   altered states of *see* ASC Jungian perception of 121-122
   shamanic control of 12, 33, 197
   shamanic state of (SSC) 15, 51-52, 60
   spirit as 114-115
conservation of sexual energy 56
core shamanism 6, 62, 68-70, 87-92
   communication with spirits of nature in 183-188
   rituals of 92-109
   soul retrieval in 155-161
cosmic zones 13
counselling, shamanic *see* shamanic counselling
Coyote tribe 21
Cuahutemoc, prince 69

dancing 59-60
   dancing the power animal 170-171
darkness 56, 98-99
death

    on denying the call of the spirits 26
    life and death in shamanic healing 137
    near-death experiences 46-47, 85
    and rebirth 28-32, 46-47
deity yoga 171
depression 27, 151
dervishes 59
Descartes, René 192
Devereux, George 26
diagnostic journeys 101, 118, 172-181, 217-218
Diószegi, V. 4
disease 140-142, 145-146
dismemberment 29, 66
dissociation 85, 151, 155
Don José (Huichol shaman) 230
Don Juan (Yaqui shaman) 15, 57, 96
Don Lucio 22
doorways between worlds 51, 62, 75
dreaming
    entering the spirit world through 15-16, 85-86
    lucid dreaming 86
    power dreams 22
    shamanic call through 22-24
drugs
    hallucinogenic 15-16, 57-59
    use of 57-59, 204
drumming 6, 7, 59-6, 67, 98
    the shaman's drum 14, 60-61

ecstasy 6, 15, 33
    see also ASC
Eliade, Mircea 4-6, 9-12, 15, 36, 50, 74, 87
    on lay shamanising 87
    on shamanic ecstasy 6, 15
    on the shaman's relationship to the spirits 10-11
    on symbolic connection between worlds 50
Emoto, Masaru 227
energy
    loss of see power loss
    sexual 56
Enet tribe 39, 45
Eskimo shamans 23, 116, 172
Evén people 138-139
exposure to extreme temperatures 56-57

fairy tales 211
fasting 55
fear 64-65, 115, 118, 203-204
    of dying 47
    spirituality as the conquest of 128-133
Frank, J. 89

Gadamer, H.G. 214
Gallegos, Stephen xii
Gestalt work 193
Gold, J. 199
grieving 101-102
Grinberg-Zilberbaum, J. 231
guardian spirits 11, 54, 68-73, 202-203, 205-206
    journeys through the eyes of the guardian spirit 784-85
    see also spirits
guided imagery 195-196
guilt 129, 143, 220
Gurdjieff, G.I. 120

Halifax, Joan 4, 39
hallucinogenic drugs 15-16, 57-59
Handleman, Don 69
Harner, Michael 6-11, 15, 87-88, 164
    on power and health 164
healing
    acquiring power for 56, 64
    community role in 142
    and the creative power of thoughts 226-229
    cross-cultural perspective on illness and healing 135-145
healing journeys 65-68, 208-217
    holistic 141, 192-193
    through imagery work 192-193
    integration of the soul 162-163
    introduction of shamanism into western healing therapy 6
    parapsychological 230-235
    rattle healing 97-98, 181-182
    rituals of 67-68, 162-163
    sacred plants for 57-59
    self-healing 42-43
    through shamanic counselling 88-92
    shamans as wounded healers 40-43
    by soul retrieval 153-154, 155-161, 232

spirit teachings on 145-147
from spirits of nature 183-187
stories and reflections 1–3, 17-18, 66, 134-135, 158-161
transformation through crisis 36-39
health 147-148
    as a matter of power 165 *see also* power loss
    psychological *see* psychological health
Hillman, James 34
Hinduism 56
Holistic healing 140-142, 191-194
Horwitz, Jonathan vii, xii, 3, 11, 69, 97, 165, 182
Huichol people 51, 57
Hutton, R. 5, 11, 25
hypnosis 52, 72, 193, 196
    self-hypnosis 224

Igjugarjuk (Eskimo shaman) 23
illness
    cross-cultural perspective on illness and healing 135-145
    'death' and rebirth 28-32, 36-37
    initiation crises of 27-28
    mental illness 32-36, 154-155, 158
    as power loss *see* power loss
    psychosomatic 142-144, 216
    as a vehicle to higher consciousness 39
    see also healing
imagery work 191-194
Ingerman, Sandra 154
initiation crises 27-28
    mental health and 32-36
    transformation through 36-40
inner sight 99
interconnectedness 129, 157, 167-170, 183-184
Inuit people 5

Jeffers, Susan 130
Jesus Christ 31-32
Jivaro people 5, 14, 16, 30, 70, 153, 164
journeys, shamanic *see* shamanic journeys
Jung, Carl G. 37, 40, 113, 120-122, 154-155, 174, 193-194
Jungian therapy 193

Kabbala 50
Kalinia people 71, 150, 168, 181

Karen shamans 156
Karinia people 151
kinesiology 171
Kleinman, Arthur 141

Lascaux caves, France 4
Lewis, I.M. 4, 10
Life
    and death in shamanic healing 137, 147
    spiritual development as purpose of 147
Lolo shamans 156
love 129, 133, 142
lower world journeys 62-68
lucid dreaming 86

magic 222-223, 227-228
    disenchantment and 235-237
Maria Sabina (Mazatec shaman) 58
Megged, Nahoum 22
memory loss 151
Menangkabau tribe 153
mental health *see* psychological health
mental preparation 95-96
mescaline 57
metaphor 189-190, 196-198
    shamanic journeys and metaphors 201-217
    transformation and metaphors 198-200
middle world journeys 80-85
Moses, spirit teacher 183-184
mushrooms, hallucinogenic 58
music 53
    see also drumming

natemä 16
nature spirits 16-17, 1183-188
near-death experiences 47, 79
Neher, A. 61
NLP (neuro-linguistic programming) 134, 189
Noll, Richard 32-34

Pachita, Doña 69, 231
Palaeolithic evidence of shamanism 4
parapsychological phenomena 230-235
Pelletier, K. 143
Perry, John 37
Peters, L.G. and Price-Williams, D. 52

peyote cactus 57
physical deprivation 55-56
Piaget, Jean 92
Piaroa tribe 5, 21
Placebo effect 225-229
places of power 61-62
plant spirits 184-186
    see also nature spirits
plants, hallucinogenic 57-59
Popov, A. 30
power animals 64, 164-171
    guardian spirits and 68-73
    power animal retrieval journeys 164-167, 232-233
power dreams 22
power loss 138-139, 16-165, 216-217
    disease as loss of energy 145-146
    through soul loss 138, 149-155, 157-158
power places 61-62
power plants 184-187
power songs 59
Prem Das (Huichol shaman) 51
psychological health 33-36
    repression and reintegration in 154-155
    transformation through crisis 36-40
psychology, western 34, 120-122, 154-155, 174
psychosis 26, 32-33
psychosomatic illness 142-144, 212
psychotherapy 89-92
purification ritual 95

rainmaking ceremony 230
Ram Dass 120
rape of the soul (soul loss) 138-139, 149-155
Rasmussen, Knud 23, 172
rattling 59, 68, 96-98
    rattle healing 98, 181-182
    the shaman's rattle 15, 96-98
rebirth 28-32
Reiki xi, 38, 134
reindeer 60
relaxation 224
religion 8-10
rituals
    of core shamanism 92-104
    dancing the power animal 170-171

    to embody a soul 162-163
    of healing 68, 162-163
    post-journey 100-104
    the power of ritual 92-93
    pre-journey 95-100
    rainmaking ceremony 230
rocks 187
Rupert, Henry (Washo shaman) 22, 69

Sabina, Maria (Mazatec shaman) 58
sacred plants 58-59
Salish tribe 70
Savone (Enet shaman) 39
schizophrenia 33-34, 144
Sedang Moi people 26
self-hypnosis 224
sensory deprivation 55-56
    sensory blocking through drumming 60-61
Sereptie (Samoyed shaman) 41, 63
sexual abstinence 56
shadow self 154-155
shamanic counselling 7, 88-92
    use of metaphor in 201-217
shamanic healing see healing
shamanic journeys
    access to power and wisdom through 229-230
    aids to entering the spirit world 15-16, 51-62
    altered states of consciousness for see ASC
    contemporary westerners and 87-88
    see also core shamanism
    diagnostic journeys 101-102, 117-118, 172-181, 218-219
    as explorations of the unconscious 194-195
    through the eyes of the guardian spirit 84-85
    flying 50, 74, 76-77, 176
    the guardian spirit and 68-73, 205-206
    see also guardian spirits
    healing journeys 65-68, 208-217
    see also healing
    lower world journeys 62-68
    mental health and 32-36
    mental preparation for 95-96
    metaphors and 201-217
    middle world journeys 80-85
    post-journey rituals 100-104

power animal retrieval journeys 163-167, 232-233
power places for 61-62
for power plants 183-188
pre-journey rituals 95-99
process of 6–7, 48-49
purpose of 6, 10-11, 48, 99-100
shamanic counselling and the understanding of 91-92
for soul retrieval 153-154, 155-161, 233
spontaneous journeys 85-86
stating the mission 98-100
transformation through 79-80, 91, 180-181, 204-217, 217-235
see also healing
upper world journeys 74-80

shamanic practices
availability of contact with spirits of nature through 16-17
imagery work 194-196
origins of shamanism 4-8, 86
religion and 8-10
rituals see rituals
the shamanic journey see shamanic journeys
spirituality and 123-133, 229-230
use of altered states of consciousness see ASC

shamanic state of consciousness (SSC) 15, 52, 60
see also ASC (altered state(s) of consciousness)

shamanic worldview 8-10, 13-17, 49-51, 76-77
the animal kingdom and shamanism 167-170
see also power animals
modern disenchantment of the world and 235-237

shamans
apprenticeship training 43-47
the call to become a shaman 21-27
contemporary shamanic counsellors 7, 89-92
see also shamanic counselling
initiatory experiences see initiation crises
lay shamanising and 87
as magicians 6
as masters of ecstasy 6, 33
as mediators between two worlds 14
as medicine men 6
motivation of 6

multiple roles of 13
transformation of soul by 71
as wounded healers 40-43

Shirokogoroff, S.M. 10
Siberian shamanism 11, 21, 25-26, 45, 49-50, 60
sickness see illness
sight 98-99
looking through the heart 104
spirit vision 23-26, 30-31, 45-46, 102-104
singing 59
sleep deprivation 56
Smith, C.M. 174
smoking, breaking the habit of 65-66
Socrates 43

souls
animalistic aspect of the soul 71, 150
beliefs concerning 114-115, 149-150
Cartesian separation of the soul and body 192
communication with 80-85
crisis generated by 36-37
multiple souls 149-150
rituals to embody a soul 162-163
soul loss 138-140, 149-155, 158-159
soul retrieval 153-154, 155-161, 233

spirit helpers 6-7, 68, 112-114
shamanic counselling as aid to contact with 89-90
see also spirit teachers

spirit intrusion 138-140, 145

spirit teachers 7, 113-114
Abraham 117
apprenticeship training by 43-46
guardian spirits as 72
Moses 183
spirits of nature as 183-188
teachings on healing 145-148
training with 44
of the upper world 76-78

spirit vision 23-26, 29-31, 44-45, 102-104
see also sight

spirit world
accessibility of 54, 183-184
aids to entering 15-16, 51-62
see also ASC
evidence for 230-235

journeys through *see* shamanic journeys
openings into the lower world 62-63
openings into the upper world 74-75
the shamanic landscape 49-51
and the unconscious mind 194-196
spirits
animal spirits 68-70
beliefs concerning 8-9, 52-53, 114-122
guardian spirits 12-13, 54, 68-73, 84-85
literary and media portrayal of 116
of nature 16-17, 183-188
nature and reality of 117-123
of the rattle 96-97, 181-183
relationship of the shaman and the spirits 10-13
of sacred plants 57-59
spirit healers 65-67, 183-188
spirit helpers *see* spirit helpers
spirit of illness 140
spirit teachers *see* spirit teachers
teaching by 43-45
tree spirits 17
spirituality 123-133, 229-230
spiritual development as purpose of life 147
story-telling 189-190, 198-200, 214
see also metaphor
sweat lodges 57
symbolism
animal symbology 166-167
archetypal 121
see also archetypes
interpreting the symbols of the journey 90-91, 100, 214-215
ritual symbolism 94, 102
of three interconnected worlds 50, 74-75
see also metaphor

Tapirapé people 5, 15, 22, 24, 46
Tart, Charles 53, 61
Telut shamans 156
temperature, exposure to extremes of 56-57
therapy
imagery work in western therapies 193-195
introduction of shamanism into western therapy 6-7, 88-89
metaphor construction 197-201

shamanic counselling and 7-8, 88-92
shamanic journeying and 195-196
the wounded healer as therapist 40-43
see also healing
thought creativity 227-229
Tiresias 99
tobacco 15-16, 25, 30, 45
transpersonal psychology 120
trauma 40, 151-154, 158-161
tree spirits 17
trees
communication with 50
hollow trees 63
tree of life 50
'world tree' 50
Tremyugan shamans 156
Tungus tribes 4, 11
Tüspüt (Yakut shaman) 27

unconscious mind
collective unconscious 121
spirit world journeys and 194
upper world journeys 74-80

vision quests 23-24, 29-31, 44-45, 102-104
visualisation 191-196

Wagley, C. 23
Walsh, Roger 31, 52, 122
Warao people 74
Wayapi people 138
Weber, Max 235
western shamanism *see* core shamanism
Wilber, Ken 34
wisdom 51-52, 86, 98-99, 120, 229-230
Witsen, Nicholas 4

yage 57
Yakut people 5, 27, 29, 74, 76, 139
yoga 171

Arvick Baghramian, currently living in Spain, received her degree in Applied Social Studies and Social Work from the University of Bradford in England. She specialized in the field of child sexual abuse and has worked with traumatized children and adults for the past twenty years, lecturing extensively on the subject and training professionals around the world. Her work with abused children compelled her to explore different therapeutic techniques, leading her to become a Play Therapist, NLP Practitioner and Eriksonian Hypnotist, and ultimately led her to Reiki, Conscious Breathing, Shamanism and the Personal Totem Pole process, all of which she has been teaching since the mid-1980's.

It was also as a result of her own personal wounding that she came to practice and teach these techniques, which are centred on self-empowerment and personal realization. Healers and spiritual teachers have often been wounded themselves, and have found their path through their own personal healing, becoming teachers that are able in their own turn to inspire others to commit to themselves and reach for a life of joy, love and freedom.

Arvick leads workshops in the UK, USA, Israel, Spain, Poland, New Zealand and the Scandinavian countries. Her commitment in directing people to achieve their full potential and to discover their true inner selves is an inspiration and her unique way of teaching as well as her personal approach and sincerity make her courses and trainings an unforgettable beginning of a new path in life.

Printed in Great Britain
by Amazon